W9-BBS-617

RHODESIA: BACKGROUND TO CONFLICT

RHODESIA:

General Editor
EDWARD WAKIN

BACKGROUND TO CONFLICT

B. VULINDLELA MTSHALI

Hawthorn Books, Inc. Publishers New York

TO MY MOTHER

 All inquiries should be addressed to Hawthorn Books, Inc., 70 Fifth Avenue, New York City 10011. This book was manufactured in the United States of America and published simultaneously in Canada by Prentice-Hall of Canada, Ltd., 1870 Birchmount Road, Scarborough, Ontario. Library of Congress Catalogue Card Number: 67–15557.

7825

RHODESIA AND THE WORLD

Since the Unilateral Declaration of Independence, Africa, the Commonwealth and the United Nations have wrestled with the problem of Rhodesia. Yet the rebels still rule, and bid fair to continue their ill-begotten reign in flagrant violation of the norms of international behaviour. Why are we in Zambia so much perturbed by their doings?

The most obvious point is what we may call the penalties of proximity. Geographically, we are contiguous to Rhodesia; economically, we are tied together. For these reasons alone we could not possibly remain indifferent to any commotion, internal or external, racking such a close neighbour.

But the greatest concern to us is the nature of the commotion itself. We in Zambia stand committed to creating a society in which men of all colours, creeds and stocks can feel at home. We abhor racialism, and will have no truck with it here at home and abroad.

Now, on November 11, 1965, Mr. Smith and his followers voluntarily opted for the role of highwaymen when they issued their UDI. Their illegal act was a blow struck for the preservation of the princely standard of living which they regard as the natural due and preserve of the few white men in the country. Theirs is the rule of a privileged, racist minority. The implications of such a state of affairs are very grave. Here I can best reiterate what I said earlier this year in the magazine *Punch:*

> . . . Rhodesia is of crucial importance, for the outcome there can determine the nature of the relationship between Europeans and coloured peoples, not only in Africa but throughout the world for many years to come. If the illegal government is permitted to succeed, then millions of coloured people are going to conclude that the West's talk of racial equality is just hypocrisy. They will believe that whenever the interests of the white man conflict with those of the coloured man, without regard to the merit of the case, the West will support the white man. Kith and kin before truth and justice. If Smith succeeds, the seeds of a future race war in southern Africa will be sown.

To prevent this horrendous war while there is still time, Zambia advocated that Britain use force. Now, this may seem out of character with one of my political beliefs: the pursuit of nonviolent solutions. But the point is that the struggle for Zambia's independence could be conducted nonviolently because we were dealing with Britain—a country susceptible to persuasion by an aroused public opinion: in short, a country with a public conscience. Rhodesia is different. There, the rebel regime flouts the opinion of mankind with pride and impunity. In our view, the only language of persuasion which such a regime best understands is force; hence our advocating it.

In doing so, however, we are also aware of the practical difficulties involved. This consideration led us to support the principle of economic sanctions. But we feared and foresaw that South Africa and Portugal would nullify them by bailing out their ally. Recent events have proved our fears justified.

To make sanctions meaningful, we, therefore, urged, and still urge, that Chapter Seven of the UN Charter be invoked so that these two countries be legally obliged to comply with sanctions or face penalties. Short of force, mandatory sanctions are our only chance of bringing down the rebels. They must be applied without delay; otherwise by dilatory action we precipitate race war.

Any book which throws light on the implications of the Rhodesian rebellion for racial harmony in southern Africa, indeed, in the whole world, does us all a great service. I welcome this one.

KENNETH D. KAUNDA
President
Republic of Zambia

State House
Lusaka, Zambia
December 28, 1966

CONTENTS

INTRODUCTION

At a time when most of Africa is free, the last strongholds of white domination persist in southern Africa—the Portuguese territories, the Republic of South Africa and Rhodesia. In Southern Rhodesia, the confrontation between a white minority and a black majority has reached its most critical point, with each side personifying a distinctive brand of nationalism.

African nationalism is a phenomenon difficult to define in political terms as precisely as its counterpart in, say, eighteenth-century France. Characteristic of both, though, is a compelling fervor manifest in the fulmination of the people against foreign rule, however benevolent. T. P. Melady quotes Daniel Manin of Venice to convey the emotional power of this feeling:

> We do not ask that Austria be humane and liberal in Italy—which, after all, would be impossible for her even if she desired; we ask her to get out. We have no concern with her humanity and her liberalism; we wish to be masters in our own house.[1]

This claim is resisted in Rhodesia by an equally strong force, best described for our purposes as settler nationalism. It emerges among those Europeans who have made their home in Africa and join forces with nationalistic ardor to retain their entrenched advantages.

As the settlers grow more and more intransigent and exclusive in their denial of African claims, the conflict between the two nationalisms becomes bitter, and an amicable outcome becomes increasingly remote. Any realist must add that the prospects of harmonious race relations in Rhodesia are as remote as those in the Republic of South Africa. In exploring the confrontation the author has tried to bring out repeatedly the close similarity between Rhodesia and South Africa. The similarity is not accidental because from the very start Rhodesian settlers openly applied to the Africans the racialist policies of South Africa.

Less well known, however, is the similarity of the African reaction in the two countries to these racialist policies. The author has tried to show how wittingly or unwittingly the Africans, suffering the same indignities from the same people, have taken the same steps to redress the wrongs done to them. As with the settlers, the Africans show about the same strong and weak points in their struggles in both countries. In focusing on the Rhodesian confrontation, the process will be examined in historical, political, economic and diplomatic terms.

The settlers are not devils, nor are the Africans angels. Far from it. The tragedy of the settlers is that they possess power and privileges, and tenaciously want to hold on to both. In defending their position, they brook no opposition and use all possible means, even despicable means. Thus the death sentence can now be passed for throwing stones at one's political opponents—at their person or property.

But more important for our purposes here is the propaganda used. It suffers from selective perception; it shows images of the African which at best are only partially true. Africans are the butt of stories and jokes purporting to prove their indolence, degeneracy and backwardness. The implicit message to the white immigrant or to the inquisitive visitor is, "You see what we have to put up with here? If we don't defend our civilized standards, then God help us all. We are doomed."

These stories and jokes demonstrate the emotional contest between the settlers and the articulate Africans. Even when lacking a basis in fact, the stories are nonetheless believed and circulated by whichever group has a score to settle with the other. Each group's image of the other group may, to a large and shocking extent, depend on such stories. Most frightening of all is the fact that this image may well govern social relationships. In other words, both blacks and whites spread stories that show their social perception of each other in the context of their conflicting roles and statuses. These stories can best be told in another setting.

The Rhodesian story that will be unfolded is richly human—sad, sordid, sometimes humorous, but, most of all, tragic. In telling it, I claim no impartiality. Politically and emotionally, I am committed to toppling the racialist regimes in my part of this small world. While the reader will have no doubts about my position, he will also have abundant material to form his own judgments. There are no liberties taken with the facts. Perhaps the best statement of my intent can be found in the favorite quotation of Arthur Goldberg, U.S. Ambassador to the United Nations. He is fond of citing the Italian historian, Gaetano Salvemini, who said: "We cannot be impartial; only intellectually honest. Impartiality is a dream, honesty a duty."

B. V. M.

September 1966

New York City

CHAPTER ONE

BEFORE THE SETTLERS CAME

The dominant elements in southern Africa hold with fanatical fervor to their feeling that civilization is the white man's gift to Africa. They visualize Africa as the Dark Continent—a wasteland devastated by warring savages, disrupted by constant chaos, crippled by human misery. The blame is placed on what is regarded as the African's inherent incapacity to overcome nature and to govern himself.

Therefore, majority rule by Africans is regarded as the road to ruin, the return to barbarism, the end of all that the white man has toiled to build. Such majority rule becomes an evil to be resisted at all cost. This is why each successive white-dominated government outdoes its predecessor in resorting to stern and drastic measures to combat African political movements. To the rulers, harshness and firmness (*kragdadigheid* as the Afrikaners call it) are popularly acclaimed political virtues, for they seem to guarantee the white man's stake in Africa and mark the difference between civilization and savagery.

However, archaeologists and historians are now busy unearthing evidence that blows the white man's case to smithereens. Their researches are systematically proving that civilizations did exist in Africa, and highly complex ones at that! The typical white settler is unnerved when he reads:

> At a time when European marines had yet to reach the Indian Ocean, or even the Bight of Benin, the kings and counsellors of Central Africa were eating from Chinese porcelain, and when Mr. Strijdom's[1] forebears drove their ox carts into the old Transvaal, they encountered men and women who were not at the beginning of a long period of civilized development, but, through times of painful dissolution, were perilously near the end of one.[2]

To suggest that the Zimbabwe Ruins near Fort Victoria are African in origin is not just unsettling to the white Rhodesian; it is treason. The very idea exacerbates white feelings as reflected by indignant letters in local newspapers. Given the politics of southern Africa, the reason for such indignation is clear. If the African had (and has) a civilization, then it was not the white man's gift; the African had long ago demonstrated his capacity to develop an advanced civilization. It is a shock to those holding myths about the white man's superiority and the black man's inferiority. The lesson of African history is added to the moral imperative of human equality, a right given by God, etched in the hearts of all men and nourished by the blood of heroes—in both African and Western history. Inexorably, that right demands that since the African is in the majority, he must necessarily rule.

In this context, it is in the settlers' interest to deny that the Zimbabwe Ruins have an African origin. It is equally in the interest of the African nationalist to prove that they do—hence the point in the impassioned plea of a Rhodesian African to a visitor from overseas: "If you want to do us a favor, find out that Zimbabwe was built by Africans!" To do so would arm the African with a potent political weapon against the minority rule of the settlers in Rhodesia. The Ruins as relics of an African era of glory, splendor, power and achievement give the lie to those who dismiss the African past as barbaric.

Since the Ruins can be seen by all Africans, whether literate or illiterate, townsmen or countryfolk, politically useful yarns and myths can be spun around them to instill a sense of pride in the African past.

Such a sense of belonging to a glorious past forges a people, gives them a sense of oneness, identity and dignity. This sense of belonging hardly flourished under colonial rule and, in fact, positive steps were taken to obliterate it. Political organizations were frowned upon. Schools injected an alien Western history into the minds of the young, making them glory in the exploits of pirates like Francis Drake and John Hawkins and sympathize with their counterparts in Eton over the loss of Jenkins' ear. After his return from London, the nationalist leader Joshua Nkomo sought to counter the symbols of British tradition by starting an organization to erect statues to the great men of the Mandebele tribe. He also began to criticize the teaching of English history to African children in Rhodesia as a deliberate device to rob them of their heritage and pride.

The situation recalls Laski's remark that education is "an art which teaches men to be deceived by the printed word." In Rhodesia, the deception consisted in denying and belittling African history. This process still continues, and has as its champions not merely settlers but even academicians of standing. This attitude is evident on all levels of Rhodesian life and is epitomized by the following statement by the second and last Prime Minister of the Federation of Rhodesia and Nyasaland, Sir Roy Welensky:

> Civilization came to this part of Africa . . . only some seventy years ago. Before then primitive tribal life alone existed; there was no money economy whatsoever, and the wheel, perhaps the basic element in civilization, was unknown.[3]

But more indicative of settler feeling in early Rhodesia is the statement by her Commissioner in Britain, R. N. Hall, who said that before Livingstone and Moffat this part of Africa had been

> . . . but a *terra incognita* wrapt in primaeval heathenism and most absolute mystery and darkness. This fair country has now been saved by the persistent policy of one man, and, what is more, it is fast being redeemed from slavery, tribal wars, raids, and wholesale murders, witchcraft and mental darkness and superstition under which its teeming populations groaned since time immemorial, and at the present time warlike and cruel potentates of this Darkest of all Africas, are stretching out hands, and not in vain—towards the benefits of civilization which they plainly see follows as a moral certainty and as truly as the day the night, wherever the flag of the Great White Mother Queen is planted.[4]

In Rhodesia, then, these crumbling Ruins, with grass sprouting out of the crags and crevices in the walls, are political dynamite. To the settler they are a symbol of his worst fears, African rule. To the African nationalist, they stand for past glory and as symbols of future power. That is why both nationalist organizations have named themselves after them. There is the Zimbabwe African People's Union (ZAPU), and the Zimbabwe African Nationalist Union (ZANU). To them the name Rhodesia is anathema; it belongs to a recent past which they want to bury. The nationalist focus now is on Zimbabwe, with Rhodes and his successors as but actors who have temporarily interrupted the drama of Zimbabwe.

But what is there about these Ruins that so excites the heart and whips up emotions? What do they mean? What manner of people produced them? When, how, what for? These questions are more easily posed than answered, for there are no written accounts. To find answers, it is necessary to reconstruct Great Zimbabwe from the scattered findings of archaeologists and historians since the discovery of the Ruins in 1868 by a hunter named Adam Renders. The best known of the two hundred ruins in Rhodesia, Great Zimbabwe lies about seventeen miles southeast of Fort Victoria in a rough stretch of woodland, near the main road linking Salisbury and Johannesburg. There are two main structures at Great Zimbabwe: one on a hill, known to Europeans as the "Acropolis"; the other, situated on level ground, has been named "the elliptical building." The "Acropolis" is strongly built, thus suggesting—as does its situation on an elevated place—a defensive function. It is an imposing structure, with massive walls thirty feet high in places and sixteen feet thick. Inside is a sacred enclosure, suggestive of a religious function.

The "elliptical building" has conical towers and thick walls.

The latter are composed of well-trimmed blocks of hard granite. Sometimes, the blocks were deliberately set at an angle for decorative effects, but generally they were fitted together in regular courses. With unrestrained admiration Howard Hensman observed in 1900: ". . . the courses of the blocks are so regular as to excite wonder in the breasts of all who behold them."[5]

The passages, recesses, gateways and platforms were all painstakingly hewn out of the local granite, and both buildings have emblems and soapstone objects in the shape of birds. Remains of gold-working utensils have also been found here and in other ruins in Rhodesia as well as in neighboring Botswana and South Africa. What the Zimbabwe gold smelters produced nobody knows, for in the 1890's adventurers ransacked the place.

These Ruins are a work of art. Clearly, the builders knew architecture, geometry and the use of pulleys, cranes and other devices for lifting weights. The occupants were skilled artisans as the utensils and decorations show. Just who were these people? The debate over this point of origin has powerful political overtones with a good number of settlers and some of the early investigators denying African origin. For their part, African nationalists insist that their ancestors built Great Zimbabwe.

The Europeans who first saw Great Zimbabwe felt it was inconceivable that such structures were put up by Africans, because they could not reconcile such art with the primitive aborigines they saw all around them. Who then built them? After a visit to Zimbabwe in 1872, a German geologist, Dr. Karl Mauch, concluded that they were built by some civilized people way back in antiquity. The "Acropolis," said the doctor, was a copy of King Solomon's temple on Mount Moriah, while the "elliptical building" was patterned after the Queen of Sheba's palace in Jerusalem. From this analysis arose the tale that Great Zimbabwe was the site of the fabulous mines of King Solomon. A veritable gold rush ensued in the 1880's, with farmers in the Transvaal deserting their plots and tearing across the Limpopo River to the Ruins in the hope that they would collect some of Solomon's gold.

According to Basil Davidson,[6] by 1900 some 114,000 gold claims were officially registered in Mashonaland and Matabeleland, most of them based on the sites of the ancient workings. The gold-seekers ransacked the ruins. Squabbles and fights over claims reached such proportions that in 1895 the British South Africa Company felt obligated to give a concession to "exploit all the ancient ruins south of Zambezi" to one company, the Ancient Ruins Company. The operations of this company were stopped in 1902; but by then irreparable damage had been done. The gold and copper objects had already been destroyed or smelted down.

Archaeologists and historians, who stand above the political controversy between the settlers and the nationalists, are not agreed on the origin of the Ruins. There are two schools of thought: one holds that the Phoenicians built Zimbabwe; the other holds that they were constructed in the Middle Ages by Africans. Holding the latter view are such renowned archaeologists as Randall-McIver, Scheebesta, G. Caton-Thompson, Roger Summers—Keeper of Antiques at the National Museum of Southern Rhodesia—and the anthropologist H. A. Wieschhoff.[7]

Some buildings have been attributed to the Barozwi people under whose hegemony the confederacy of the Seshona-speaking Africans[8] flourished in the eighteenth century before being destroyed in the nineteenth by invaders from Zululand. Summers says that the original inhabitants are thought to have been the "forefathers of the present Basuto and other people now living in the Union and the High Commission Territories."[9]

This view finds added support from a Catholic priest, Mongameli Mabona. In *Presence Africaine*[10] he suggested that *zimbabwe* is a distorted Nguni word; it should be *zimbiwambiwe,* a short form for *kwazintaba zimbiwambiwe,* meaning mountains full of mines. However, Mabona has yet to show how the other more widely held meanings are wrong. The meaning one gives to the word *zimbabwe* indicates one's theory about what the buildings and their occupants were noted for. Thus for Mabona, the place was famous for gold mining; as proof he can point to the utensils. For Summers, however, the primary function seems to have been connected with religion because in Seshona *mazimbabwe* means the graves of chiefs. People used to come to the graves to propitiate the spirits of the dead chiefs and to ask them for advice and help. There is a basis for this contention because the ruins indeed have a sacred enclosure. Summers adds that the size and importance of Great Zimbabwe entitle it to be regarded as the capital of the Mashona people whose king, the Monomotapa, ruled over extensive domains in the fourteenth and fifteenth centuries.

To reconcile these views, we can take a middle road. Gold, religion and politics are not mutually exclusive, as is evident from the practices of the Ashanti of the former Gold Coast. It is not farfetched to suggest that in the case of Great Zimbabwe all three functions were involved, each about equal in importance to the other.

While the exact age of the Ruins is uncertain, two pieces of wood discovered in 1950 have given a clue. Tests conducted in London and Chicago showed that they were cut from a hard tree between A.D. 500 and 700. The Ruins were, therefore, built about this time—an interesting date, for this is the era known in the history of Europe as the Dark Ages.

Both the original buildings and the additions attributed to the Barozwi testify to the existence of an era of peace, prosperity, administrative ability and scientific advancement. Details are available from the time of the Mashona invasion in the fifteenth century when the Portuguese were starting their settlements of the eastern coast of Africa. The Portuguese kept records of the stories of this powerful state south of the Zambezi—stories of fabulous riches which excited Europe right up to the nineteenth century. The Portuguese called this state the "Empire of Benametapa," ruled by the *Monomotapa*—this being their rendering of the native title for the ruler. The first European to visit the Empire was Antonio Fernandez, who was sent by the Portuguese government in 1514 to investigate the source of the gold which was reaching Sofala near Beira in present-day Mozambique. Some three years later we hear it said by a countryman of his that the Monomotapa "is the lord of an exceeding great country. It runs far inland. It extends to the Cape of Good Hope and to Mozambique."

At this time the Makaranga people ruled the kingdom, and had their capital and royal cemetery at Zimbabwe. They seem to have been noted for their prominence in the "arts of peace"—agriculture, weaving, pottery, carving and iron smelting.[11]

What was the Zimbabwe-Monomotapa culture like? Wieschhoff has summarized the findings of earlier writers and explorers.[12] The main part of the ruler's court consisted of wives, literally thousands of them. Of these, nine—the majority being his own sisters and relatives—had the rank of queen and special names. All had the power of life and death over their subjects and they had a powerful voice in the succession to the throne. Nobody could become king unless he had received the approval of the council of women, even though he had been appointed by the Monomotapa to succeed him, as custom prescribed.

The Monomotapa had to be free of physical defect. In case of sickness or bodily disfiguration, he had to take poison together with his chief wives who were to keep him company in the next world. (It is said that the king ruling in 1635 lost an eye and was asked to appoint a successor. When he refused, a revolt broke out.) The Monomotapa was the supreme feudal lord, owning everything in the country, and his subjects received their possessions from him as a loan. An awe-inspiring figure, he could summarily condemn to death and order instant execution. He made sacred fire, which was distributed to his chiefs and vassals as a symbol of authority. He sowed the first seeds and harvested the first crops, and on his physical well-being depended the health and fertility of his lands. His whole life was shrouded in mystery. "No ordinary person was allowed to see him, and when he gave interviews he was hidden behind a screen, or when walking outside his court, his arrival was announced so that his subjects could disappear."[13] Nor could he be seen eating or drinking. On the very few occasions when he granted an audience, special rituals had to be observed by all, Europeans included. His life then was a secluded and secret one; so was his death. How did anybody succeed to such a powerful and frightening position? As Professor Roland Oliver of the London School of Oriental and African Studies tells us, "Succession was elective within the royal family, and herein lay the principal weakness of all the African kingdoms of this type, for succession disputes gave rise to splits especially under the influence of outside pressures."[14] Later this weakness was shrewdly exploited by the Portuguese and the kingdom collapsed.

The kingdom was administered by many officials, each having a specific task to do either in the royal court or in the country at large. The leading officials included the chancellor of the state (prime minister), governor, chief drummer, chief witch doctor. The Monomotapa's civil service has been compared to the bureaucracy of the Kabaka of Buganda.

Like the Roman Empire, the kingdom declined because of both internal and external forces. In the sprawling kingdom, dynastic rivalries grew so unmanageable that they led to destructive wars which overtaxed the fabric of the feudal society. As a result, the Portuguese without much opposition were able to undermine the state. The Portuguese first obtained a monopoly of the maritime trade with India, but the merchants resented their exorbitant rates and stopped placing orders. Then the Portuguese forced the Monomotapa to grant them a monopoly of the gold mines in exchange for keeping him secure in his position. But the Portuguese violated the agreement by encouraging rival leaders and by interfering with coastal trade. The Monomotapa then forbade his subjects to take away gold. If they discovered a mine, they had to cover the spot with earth and set a bough on it to warn others to avoid it on pain of death.

Why such a penalty? The Dominican monk Joao dos Santos gives the answer in his *Ethiopia Oriental* written in 1619: "This severitie is used to keep the Mines from the knowledge of the Portugals, lest covetous desire thereof might cause them to take away their Countrey."[15]

The Monomotapa had good reason to fear for his safety, for the coming of the Portuguese was a mixed blessing. In 1607 they helped the Monomotapa Gatsi Rusere quell a rebellion. But through their help they

> . . . had proved that whoever employed European fire-arms could become masters of south-east Africa. By interfering in the internal affairs of Monomotapa they had saved the Paramount Chief from overthrow and stayed the disintegration of his kingdom. His conditional grant to them of the mines, though not perhaps valid by native law, seemed to them just and reasonable reward for their exertions on his behalf.[16]

But this was not the end of Portuguese interference. Professor G. R. Boxer of London University tells us that they also

> . . . intervened in a Makaranga succession dispute and enthroned a paramount chief who acknowledged himself as a vassal of the king of Portugal and became a Christian with his wife and family. The ensuing decades were the golden age of the Portuguese in East Africa, when their traders traversed the lands of the Monomotapa "as securely as if they were in the safest lands of Europe."[17]

Thus, the Portuguese experience was the prelude to the two traumatic experiences that shook the Monomotapa Kingdom in the ensuing two centuries. First, there were the invasions by African tribes, especially the militaristic Nguni and their tribal offshoot, the Mandebele. Second, there was the arrival of the white settlers under Rhodes who delivered the *coup de grace* to tribal independence.

CHAPTER TWO

THE CONQUEST OF RHODESIA

Unlike the Mashona, who trace their origins in Rhodesia to the Middle Ages, the martial Mandebele entered Rhodesian territory in the last century as a by-product of tribal wars and European pressures. Today, 750,000 Mandebele and 2,750,000 Mashona constitute the two major tribal groupings in the territory, joint heirs of a troubled past and victims of an uncertain present.

The nineteenth-century experience began in Zulu wars involving complicated tribal relations and ended in dominance by land-hungry white settlers. The towering figure on the African scene was the Zulu king, Shaka, who emerged victorious from an epochal nineteenth-century tribal war in Zululand. His victory radically changed the map of Africa from the Cape to mainland Tanganyika. In the wholesale reshuffling of tribal entities, the Mandebele were driven north. They then subdued the Mashona, their current majority partner in Rhodesia.

This must be seen in the context of the interlocking tribal groupings and the place of the Mandebele in the Nguni constellations of the early nineteenth century. Before Shaka's time there was no such thing as a Zulu nation; rather there were three major groupings of equally powerful units or clans: the Qwabe, the Mthethwa, and the Ndwandwe.

The issue was joined between the ruler of the Ndwandwe, Zwide kaLanga, and Shaka, who had risen to leadership of the Mthethwa clan from his position as leader of the small Zulu clan under the Mthethwa. A military genius and a skillful politician, Shaka confronted the military power of Zwide by organizing an effective army of his Zulu tribesmen. Shaka the general defeated superior enemy forces; Shaka the ruler set about increasing his kingdom.

With Zwide's defeat, the Ndwandwe scattered in a dispersal involving its three subclans: the Swazi under Zwangendaba, the Shangane under Soshangane, and the Khumalo under his son-in-law, Mashobane. Soshangane and Zwangendaba crossed into Rhodesia and defeated the Mashona. Part of Zwangendaba's group later settled in Zambia, Malawi and Tanzania. They still can be traced by their surnames. (For example, the Zambian Minister of Mines and Cooperatives bears the surname Zulu.)

While the others fled, Mashobane remained behind and bided his time. But disaster was soon upon him. He failed in a military campaign and Shaka executed him. Mzilikazi, his son, then took off northward with his followers known as the Mandebele. To keep his forces at full strength, he recruited young men from the tribes he conquered on the way. Finally, he settled down in what is now the Transvaal. But not for long. The Boers soon drove him across the Limpopo River into present-day Matabeleland, where, after defeating the Mashona, he reigned until his death in 1868.

Mzilikazi's son and successor, Lobengula, pursued an expansionist policy, taking advantage of the decline of the neighboring Shona-speaking peoples. Victory came quickly, for the opposing Mashona chiefs had lost much of their power. Following his father's policy, Lobengula reinforced his troops by recruiting from the conquered areas. He consolidated his kingdom by encouraging intermarriage, while at the same time leaving the conquered societies intact. He did this so that they could produce food and cattle, which he would take when he next raided these people.

Some historians allege that the Mashona were held in slavery. Far from it. What the Mandebele did was to continue Shaka's practice of taking women for his harem and young men for his army so that the crossing of blood would secure him from attack by the vanquished and give him their loyalty. This was well understood by the first white people to visit Zululand. Shaka is reputed to have had two white wives.[1]

This Nguni practice worked. The numerically superior Mashona never banded together to oust the enemy, and today it is misleading to speak of tribal animosity and the possibility of civil war—as did that South African writer Stuart Cloete in his letter to *The New York Times*, November 30, 1965. The Zimbabwe Africans never have been split according to tribal ties. In vain have successive settler regimes tried to fan the flames of tribalism. Indeed, the Ndebele Nkomo and ZAPU are strongest in Salisbury, in the heart of Mashonaland.

Since the Mandebele dominated the territory comprising present-day Rhodesia from the 1840's, the white man encountered the Mandebele rulers Mzilikazi and Lobengula—and puzzled over their personalities and policies. The writings of the first Europeans give the impression that Mzilikazi was a baffling figure. He was at times kind, jocular and frank; other times he would be rude, evasive and suspicious. We must take into account who these first Europeans were: elephant hunters, traders, gold prospectors and missionaries coming up from the Transvaal. While on his guard, Mzilikazi maintained excellent relations with them, potential enemies though they were. He was fond of the missionary Robert Moffat. David Livingstone is full of praises for him. The hunter Adam Renders, who discovered the Great Zimbabwe, felt so much at home that he left his family in the Transvaal and settled down with the daughter of a local chief.[2] But why was Mzilikazi sometimes cold and suspicious? Himself a victim of pressure from the Boers in South Africa, Mzilikazi knew the tactics of European infiltration. ". . . he had heard how first the missionaries had come and then the traders and last the soldiers, how one chief after another had ended in despair or exile or had lived on as a vassal with his power reduced."[3]

This suspicion and wariness was passed on to his son Lobengula, who in his own graphic and inimitable style put the matter in these words:

> Did you ever see a chameleon catch a fly? . . . The chameleon gets behind the fly and remains motionless for some time; then he advances very slowly and gently, first putting forward one leg and

then another. At last, when well within reach, he darts his tongue and the fly disappears. England is the chameleon and I am that fly.[4]

In the meantime, Lobengula was receiving and entertaining all sorts of comers and giving away nothing. He amused himself on one occasion by stroking a Jesuit priest's beard which he called a lion's mane.[5]

The Mandebele had reason to fear the chameleon. They blocked the natural path of British expansion, as conceived by the rulers of the Cape, who thought in terms of a road from the Cape to Cairo. In the east, the Transvaal Boers were inveterate enemies of the British and would grant no free passage; in the west lay a desert, blazing hot and inhospitable. The only way open was a strip of land called the "missionaries' road," lying between Bechuanaland (now Botswana) and the Transvaal and leading directly to Lobengula's territory. Cecil John Rhodes, the personification of the chameleon, soon dubbed this road to the north the "Suez Canal." But Lobengula was the Nasser whose permission was needed for the right to pass through.

Rhodes realized that the only way of securing that free passage to the north was effective occupation of King Lobengula's lands. A conflict was, therefore, inevitable. Despite the healthy respect that he had for the fighting prowess of the Mandebele, Rhodes was hopeful of victory. He was cocky—after all, the Boers and the British had defeated the formidable Zulus both on paper and on the field of battle. On paper, they had hoodwinked the kings into giving away their lands; and on the battlefield, they had routed them. Given the right circumstances and the right people and a little bit of luck, he could get his way. Without delay, he set about making plans.

Meanwhile, Lobengula had been so pestered by gold-seeking adventurers that in 1869, in the hope of keeping them away, he granted one concession for digging in the Tati area near Bechuanaland. This was later accompanied by a commission to the concessionaire company to make laws in this area since, in his own words, "the laws of my country are not suitable for the government of Europeans." But this did not put an end to the gold rush, for two reasons. First, the findings of Mauch had given rise to the fable that Great Zimbabwe was the site of the rich mines of King Solomon. Second, in the 1880's during the scramble for Africa, Central Africa was eagerly sought by Portugal, by Germany, and by the Boers whose reading of the Old Testament told them that the promised land was not confined to the Transvaal. At this time the British Treasury was not very enthusiastic about acquiring colonies which might prove to be, in the words of Disraeli, "millstones round our necks."

But Cecil John Rhodes saw no millstones, only visions. A "tall, lanky, anemic, fair-haired boy" of poor health, he was a seventeen-year-old son of a parson and came to South Africa in 1870 for his health. Very quickly he got well, and by his thirties had amassed a fortune from diamond-mining at Kimberley. But money held no particular attraction for him; it was the power it gave him for his political ambitions that mattered. At Oxford, Kipling had imparted to him a love for extending the British Empire. To Rhodes, the Union Jack was destined to fly throughout the whole world, ushering in such progress as the British alone could bring. In fact, his grand design, contained in one of his wills, even included the "ultimate recovery of the United States."

Such a man could not be a disinterested spectator in the

scramble for Africa. On the contrary, he saw himself as duty bound to act quickly to outwit and forestall the other parties whose covetous eyes were already fixed on Central Africa. He was also confident, for he knew the frailties of men. In his Kimberley bargaining for diamonds he had long discovered the power of money over men, however strong their principles were. He was prepared, as he put it, to "square" an opponent through hard bargaining backed by money and, if need be, by a *fait accompli.*

In January, 1888, Rhodes was stunned by the news that King Lobengula had signed a treaty with the Transvaal Boers. But he was not short of a solution. At this time John Moffat—son of Robert Moffat, who had been a trusted friend of Mzilikazi—was an agent of the British High Commissioner to the court of Lobengula. The latter trusted him; so did Rhodes, an old friend of his. Together they prevailed upon Lobengula to rescind the treaty and replace it with a treaty whereby he would not make agreement with foreign states or cede his lands "without the previous knowledge and sanction" of the British High Commissioner to South Africa. Lobengula agreed because he thought this would free him from the pressures of foreign agents, apart from the British. He trusted John Moffat and thought that through him he would be able to strike the best bargain with the British, whom Lobengula regarded as unreliable. In the words of the British Commissioner for Bechuanaland, Sir Sidney Shippard:

> . . . he [Lobengula] knows how England, after the fairest promises, handed over 750,000 unwilling natives to the Boers whom they dread and detest. . . . He is sharp enough and farsighted enough to understand that the English alliance might be his best

card if only he could trust the English, but there's the rub. England has a bad name in South Africa for breaking faith with natives.[6]

But with the help of a councillor, Shippard and Moffat allayed the fears of the King and persuaded him to give a concession to three men representing Rhodes: Charles Rudd, Rhodes' old partner from Kimberley and a graduate of Cambridge; Rochfort Macguire, a barrister and a product of Oxford; and Francis Thompson, a South African, specially brought along as an expert on the customs and language of the Mandebele. On October 30, 1888, Lobengula granted the concession, now known as the Rudd Concession, whereby he gave exclusive mining rights in his domains to Rhodes. In exchange, he and his successors and heirs were to receive one hundred pounds a month in perpetuity, one thousand rifles, ammunition and an armed steamboat on the Zambezi River. The last item was Rhodes' masterstroke, one which Stanley had also successfully used in the Congo.[7]

Unwittingly, King Lobengula had signed his own death warrant; the chameleon had now come within striking distance. He thought (and was so advised by his friends, councillors and missionaries alike) that he was merely granting a mining concession and not surrendering sovereignty over his lands. But to Rhodes and his friends this is exactly what the Concession meant. No sooner had the deal been made public than other concession seekers pointed this out to King Lobengula. He was puzzled, and regretted his decision. Then he was astonished when he received a letter from Queen Victoria saying that "a king gives a stranger an ox, not his whole herd of cattle." This letter made him think that the Concession could be interpreted to mean that he had given more than he had intended. Indeed, a rereading of the document to him by other missionaries convinced him that he had been tricked. In September 1889, he canceled the Concession and sent emissaries to England to inform the Queen that the agreement with Rhodes was now invalid. But the latter completely discredited him, and went ahead with his schemes.

With the Rudd Concession in his possession, Rhodes applied to Her Majesty's Government for permission to form a company under Royal Charter to develop the mineral resources, extend railways and generally bring "progress" to the area then known as Zambezia. A request to extend the Empire through a commercial company rather than by direct annexation by the Crown may seem strange, but political conditions in Britain made such a course possible. First of all, as Disraeli had expressed it, Britain was loath to add to her already heavy colonial expenses unless there were clear prospects of immediate gain. Moreover, the crises over Irish Home Rule had proved imperial ventures to be hazardous undertakings.[8] Also, Britain feared that direct intervention would provoke the Boers and invite another war. Therefore, she decided that expansion, where necessary and likely to be profitable, was to be through her Cape Colony. The result was that policy tended to be "made in Cape Town and merely approved or amended in London."[9]

A further reason for the colonization of Zambezia (later to be Rhodesia) by the Cape Colony was the belief that this area was as rich in gold as the Johannesburg area and would therefore draw white settlers. The British High Commissioner to South Africa, Sir Hercules Robinson, "believed it to be vital to imperial supremacy in south Africa that the colonists should be loyalists from the Cape, and not Transvaalers or

Boers; for whoever developed and controlled this region would be adding weight either to the republicans or to the colonial side of the South African balance."[10]

Since the Cape Colony was too poor to undertake such a project, Rhodes' proposal was especially attractive to the British Prime Minister Lord Salisbury (the grandfather of the present Marquis). He thought it would ensure "the reality of British control without the odium and the expense of annexation."[11] Moreover, in supporting Rhodes both Salisbury and Knutsford, the Colonial Secretary, "expected high political dividends. They extended the empire through the chartered company, not primarily to increase British trade, but to shape the intrinsically neutral movement of commercial development and colonization to their own political design."[12] This design concerned Britain's diplomatic strategy and security as a world power.

Getting the charter, however, was no easy task for Rhodes. First, he had to keep up the pretense that the Rudd Concession authorized him to exercise sovereign power—hence he had to discredit King Lobengula's emissaries and letter to the Queen. Second, he had to silence the humanitarian societies, who opposed the granting of administrative power to a commercial company out of fear that the company would mistreat the native population and fight the Mandebele. Right though its cause was, the opposition failed to solidify and move public opinion as Rhodes carried the day with his skilled lobbying. His strategy in pursuit of the charter was as fascinating and instructive as it was successful. On October 29, 1889, he received the charter authorizing his British South Africa Company (BSAC) over the next twenty-five years to "acquire by any concession, agreement, grant or treaty, all or any rights, interests, authorities, jurisdiction and powers of any kind or nature whatever, including powers necessary for the purpose of government and the preservation of public order."

In the meantime his representative to the court of King Lobengula, Dr. Starr Jameson, had obtained from the King permission for the gold-seekers to pass through his lands to Mashonaland—a permission which Jameson falsely represented in Cape Town as sanction to occupy Mashonaland. On the basis of Jameson's report, the British government granted Rhodes permission to march his men to take Mashonaland in the name of the Queen.

In the development of race relations in Rhodesia, this group of men—the Pioneer Column, as the history books call them—played a major part. Out of two thousand applicants from all the districts of South Africa and from the Boers and the British, Rhodes selected some two hundred young men between the ages of twenty-five and thirty to start the settlement of Mashonaland. With various skills and backgrounds for both town and country life, these men were each promised fifteen gold claims, and a farm of three thousand acres. Rhodes chose to recruit from what he called the "two races" so that "if anything should go wrong, every element in the electorates of Natal and of the Cape would join in the clamour for England to intervene . . . and if things went well, 'the two races' would be joined in partnership."[13] All the Pioneers were well acquainted with South Africa's thinking on matters of race; thus one of them described the Mandebele as "a nation of ferocious savages, whose all-pervading, all-absorbing instinct is blood and rapine." Views of this sort were (and still are) common in South Africa. Inevitably, Rhodesia was from the start as much tainted with them as was South Africa, where the Africans were being victimized by both the Boers and the British.

In the case of the Boers, their racial views were set forth in the Piet Retief Manifesto, an 1837 document stating the reasons for their departure from the Cape Colony, which they regarded as too liberal. Among other things, the Manifesto said: "We are resolved, wherever we go, that we will uphold the just principles of liberty; but, whilst we will take care that no one shall be held in a state of slavery, it is our determination to maintain such regulations as may suppress crime, and preserve proper relations between master and servant."[14] This declaration of liberty is oddly phrased: the masters were determined to be judges of what constituted crime and proper relations. They say nothing about safeguarding the rights of the servants against the masters. The point here is that the Boers were leaving the Cape Colony because of the "ungodly equality" which British laws fostered between black and white. Rejecting the British view, the constitution of their South African Republic as a consequence explicitly stated that in both Church and State there was to be no equality between black and white. The British tradition, while less forthright, practically had the same effect as that of the Boers. Rhodesia, thus, inherited both traditions, and has ever since closely copied South Africa's segregationist practices.

Therefore on September 12, 1890, when the Pioneers hoisted the Union Jack at Fort Salisbury (named after the British Prime Minister), the fate of the Africans was sealed and the stage set for the troubles now racking this country. Realizing what the Pioneers were up to, King Lobengula in utter dismay and disbelief remarked, "I thought you came to dig gold, but it seems you have come to rob me of my people and my country as well." To the Queen he sent a plea for help, but it was too late. Rhodes had gobbled up the country—hence the poignant question of a Ndebele chief to a white man: "Have you got a brother named Rhodes who eats a whole country for breakfast?"

In retrospect, it is likely that the very first contact with the Europeans signaled the doom of the Ndebele rule—with the gun destined to decide the issue. But the trickery and the duplicity which Rhodes used to acquire the lands of King Lobengula incense the African nationalists far more than did the defeats on the battlefield in 1893 and 1896. African nationalist feeling is based on an "if only" argument. The nationalists argue that if only King Lobengula had not been deceived by the unconscionable gold-seekers, but had instead heeded the advice of his younger soldiers that he wipe out the insistent and pestering prospectors while they were still few and weak, the outcome would have been different.

To support their contention, the nationalists point to the morbid fear which the early settlers had of the Mandebele fighters. Even the fully armed Pioneer Column with an escort of five hundred policemen was so obsessed with the possibility of ambush during the march that at night they could not distinguish between the cry of a hungry or lonely wolf and that of a Ndebele scout telling his colleagues to swoop down on the benighted Column. But the King had promised not to molest the supposedly gold-seeking people, and kept his word even when doubtful of their intentions, for, as he said, "The word of a King is surrounded by a wall." One can then legitimately ask those who regard the settlers as civilized and the African as savage whether this sordid deal by the Pioneers of whom they are so proud does not undermine their heroic myths. Indeed, the Judicial Committee of the Privy Council—the highest court of appeal in the British Empire—ruled in 1918 that legally the King had been robbed of his lands, and that these now belonged to the British Crown rather than to the BSAC. Militarily, however, he had long lost. Realizing his error of judgment, he belatedly fought the Pioneers in 1893, and was mercilessly mowed down. Rather than surrender, he burned his residence, took to flight and died on the run. With him, as with one of his Mashona predecessors, the Monomotapa, went the secrets of many gold-laden places on his lands, such as the Zimbabwe Ruins. Even after granting concessions, he was opposed to having the Ruins disturbed by gold hunters.[15]

The causes of the two uprisings against the settlers (who call the second a rebellion) throw considerable light on race relations. The term itself, *rebellion,* is a misnomer since the settlers were not the lawfully constituted authority. Instead, as the sordid history of the Concession shows, they had usurped the King's powers. But because they felt superior, and because they wanted to justify to public opinion in Britain their shooting of the Africans, they had to appear in the right, and the Africans in the wrong—as rebels. As John Harris angrily observed in his book, denouncing settler duplicity and lies:

> It has hitherto been held that the wicked Matabele, under a still more savage king, committed such heinous crimes and created such widespread terror and slaughter that the Chartered Company with an executive personnel normally incapable of telling an untruth or of harming a mouse was in sheer defence compelled to oppose the Matabele hordes.[16]

Actually, Rhodes was ruthlessly realizing a dream: the occupation of Mashonaland and Matabeleland. For him this was "what yachts, mansions, and mistresses were for contemporary tycoons like Jay Gould and Rockefeller. Lonely, without a wife or children, he regarded his personal colonialism as a combination of mistress, son, hobby and luxury all rolled into one."[17] This possessive feeling was heightened in 1895 by having this huge territory, three times the size of England and Wales, named after him. As a result, he brooked no opposition to his project, and was "impatient of legal niceties and administrative procedure,"[18] especially in matters affecting the African. With himself now doubling as head of the British South Africa Company and Prime Minister of the Cape Colony from which the BSAC was directed, the settlers under Jameson were guaranteed a free hand in their treatment of the African immediately after they had hoisted the Union Jack.

In 1896, the Mashona took to arms with their former enemies, the Mandebele, to the surprise of the settlers. In settler circles, the Mashona were widely regarded, in the words of Nurse Elsa Green, as "cowardly and contemptible, . . . sunk in vice and immorality"[19] and contemptuous of manual work. Nurse Green tells us that to put them on the path of righteousness, "A hut tax—that excellent and necessary institution—was levied. To pay this the Mashonas must work. They hate work, and although they soon became aware of the advantages of money, they could not throw off their habitual laziness to gain it."[20] Therefore, in her view, they rose because hatred of work is close to hatred of those who enforce it.

It is true that the hut tax was particularly galling and humiliating to both the Mandebele and the Mashona because it wrenched them from their beloved homes, friends, cattle and fields, and forced them to work for a pittance in the mines and on the farms of the settlers. Like Bambada kaMancinza, who in 1906 rose in Zululand, they resented and abhorred such labor. Laziness had nothing to do with the issue, since the Africans never invited or implored the settlers to make them industrious. Imbued with their ideas of progress and civilization, the settlers on the contrary saw things in a different light. They were convinced that the African was incorrigibly and incurably lazy. Moreover, before the settler era, the African's life was, in Hobbes' words "short, nasty and brutish." The settlers, therefore, felt it to be their mission to force the African for his own good into the ranks of the civilized; hence the introduction of "that excellent and necessary institution," the hut tax.

One of the major grievances of the Mashona was the company's maladministration. Some native commissioners were ruthless in implementing the company's policies. The Mashonaland-based missionary, John White, mentions the case of one such official who was found guilty of procuring a girl for immoral purposes. Of this man White writes: "He shortly after left the country; yet so trivial seemed the offence that within nine months he was back again, and held an official position in the force raised to punish the rebels."[21]

The Mashona and Mandebele policemen who served under the native commissioners were yet another source of dissatisfaction. Says White: "These fellows, previously the most arrant cowards, once they are invested with a little authority and armed with a rifle, develop into the cruellest of tyrants. . . . They never scruple to use their position to get almost anything they wish."[22] The policemen demanded women, beer, meat. In enforcing the hut tax, they took away cattle—the proudest possession of the African, the symbol of his status and wealth. African though they were, their fellowmen identified them with the enemy. Even today, police brutality in Rhodesia and in South Africa is as sore a point as it is in Harlem, further resentment being caused by the later use of these policemen as spies.[23]

Apart from company officials, the settlers themselves created resentment. They not only bought "native mistresses," thereby making White warn the government that it would soon be "confronted with the most serious social problem," but also took the law into their own hands. Cases of flogging the workers and of withholding wages were quite common. Finally, locust plagues and cattle diseases were attributed to the white men by the witch doctors, who advised the Mashona that the only way to end all their troubles was to wipe out the settlers.

In words equally applicable to Rhodesia of the 1960's, White ended his letter by saying: "At present the land is under a dark cloud; confusion and strife reign everywhere. Let those in authority face the position with brave and honest hearts. Where corruption and injustice are found, let them be swept away, and let the foundations of this new colony be laid in righteousness and truth, then we feel sure a bright and successful future awaits us."[24]

But this was a voice crying in the wilderness. As White himself said, if anybody suggested that the African was being ill treated, the settlers curtly replied that this was "a cowardly and wicked lie." The Boer element among the settlers frowned on missionaries; after all, had their fathers, when quitting the Cape Colony a few decades earlier, not complained in the Manifesto "of the unjustifiable odium which has been cast upon us by interested and dishonest persons, under the cloak of religion, whose testimony is believed in England, to the exclusion of all evidence in our favor"?[25] These are words with a familiar ring to enlightened contemporary clergymen like Michael Scott, George Houser, Canon Collins, Bishops Huddleston and Pike, and Archbishop Hurley.

The wrongs were deliberately not redressed. Since Occupation Day, the settlers had been preparing to "smash the Matabele" (Mandebele). They felt that their properties in Mashonaland were not safe unless the Mandebele were crushed, even though the King had guaranteed their safety so long as they sought gold and nothing else. But they wanted more. On behalf of the BSAC, Jameson began recruiting soldiers for the invasion of Lobengula, and drew up a document on August 14, 1893, setting out the condition of service. Two of the most revealing clauses stated that "each member will be entitled to mark out a farm of 6000 acres in any part of Matabeleland," and that "The loot shall be divided one-half to the BSA Company and the remainder to officers and men in equal shares.[26] Evident here is the intention to deprive the Mandebele of their lands. Just as revealing and a little amusing is this news report in the *Mashonaland Times* of July 20, 1893:

> SUNDAY—Rev. Sylvester as military chaplain, holds service after parade for inspection of arms. The rev. gentleman stood on ammunition cases and said that the sons of Ham would all be cleared out. He considered the Chartered Company had not quite forgotten its duty. . . . Cricket match in afternoon."[27]

The Mandebele and Mashona were crushed in 1896, and since then the settlers have maintained law and order without a fight. Indeed, until the 1960 riots in Salisbury and Gwelo and Bulawayo, they boasted that they had never fired another shot in anger.

CHAPTER THREE

RULE BY COMPANY CHARTER

As the nineteenth century was ending, the echo in London of gunfire in Africa forced the British Colonial Office to discard its reluctance to intervene in the new colony of Rhodesia. First, it was the Jameson Raid of 1895 in which Rhodes and Jameson tried to annex the Transvaal by force, only to be turned back by the Boers.[1] Then there were the 1896 and 1897 uprisings by the Mandebele and the Mashona.

Rhodes was forced to resign as Cape Premier, a move which enabled him to spend more time on his dream of African glory. From London, Sir Richard Martin was dispatched to become Resident Commissioner in the Rhodesian capital, Salisbury. There he was to be the eyes and ears of the Colonial Office, with veto powers over the company's Administrator. To South Africa, the Colonial Office sent the experienced official Sir Alfred Milner, to become High Commissioner with jurisdiction over both South Africa and Rhodesia. But for all practical purposes, Rhodesia was still dominated by the settlers and the British South Africa Company (BSAC), whose views did not necessarily agree with those of the British government.

One of Milner's most important moves in Rhodesia was to introduce in the 1898 Order-in-Council a clause saying, "No conditions, disabilities or restrictions shall, without the previous consent of the Secretary of State, be imposed upon the natives by ordinances which do not equally apply to persons of European descent, save in the supply of arms, ammunition and liquor." The settlers were incensed because, in dealing with the Africans, they now had to rely on the Resident Commissioner, who in their view was likely to be soft on the "native question." In point of fact, their fears were unfounded, since this provision did not change the existing drastic inroad into the African's rights in the form of land apportionment, the hut tax and the passes. In effect, the provision was just legal fiction, hardly ever enforced in Rhodesian history.

What further annoyed the settlers was Milner's prevention of other Jameson Raids by removing control of the armed forces from the BSAC and putting them in the hands of the Resident Commissioner. This change did not mean much either. Since they were made up of and commanded by settlers, the Crown could not take the loyalty of the armed forces for granted in case of, say, another African uprising. This was indeed an exceptional situation, for Britain normally sent her own troops to the colonies. Britain held such light rein on the armed forces that she readily handed power over them back to the settlers when Rhodesia became a self-governing colony in 1923.

But to satisfy the settlers, Milner, through the same Constitution, created a Legislative Council consisting of five members nominated by the BSAC and four elected by the settlers, thus guaranteeing BSAC control. For Rhodes this was a first welcome step toward self-government, which he had plainly told the shareholders was his aim for the territory: "When our territory becomes filled with white people, there is one thing we shall insist on—namely, self-government."

The voting arrangement was taken directly from the Cape, where few Africans could qualify to vote because of the education or wealth requirements. Under Milner's Constitution, the remarkable thing is that those Africans who were entered as voters were not even local. They were Xhosas, Zulus, Basutos and Fingos who had emigrated from South Africa, usually with their white employers under a scheme organized by Rhodes. By 1911, fifty-one of them were on the voters' roll. For the Rhodesian Africans, however, there was no provision made because, in the words of the Native Affairs Committee of Enquiry of 1910–1911, "there can be no doubt that the natives of this territory are as yet quite unfit for the exercise of any legislative franchise."[2] It, therefore, recommended that their interests be looked after by the Secretary for Native Affairs, appointed with the approval of the High Commissioner. Of one of these officials (Marshall Clarke), R. N. Hall said that his "long and intimate experience and successful treatment of native matters in South Africa is a sufficient guarantee to the Home Government [in Britain] that the interests of the natives will be adequately safeguarded."[3]

In this way, Rhodesia was copying South Africa's policy of

keeping the native in his place; this became the task of the Department of Native Affairs. It is ironic that the vote was given only to Africans from South Africa. This was done as a concession to the English element and to Milner. The Boers, who were totally opposed to the idea, agreed only because they were privately assured that the Africans would never be strong enough to determine electoral results; nor would they be able to elect any of their own people to the Council. Indeed, no African ever sat in the Rhodesian Parliament before 1962.

As shown earlier, the settlers' attitude to the African was governed by their feeling of "cultural superiority." Just as important, though, was the economic factor. From the very start, the settlers employed Africans in the towns, households, mines and on farms for unskilled and menial tasks. The Africans from South Africa were better off because of their skills; for example, they drove tractors and automobiles at higher wages than their local counterparts.[4] The native Africans, meanwhile, were regarded purely as temporary sojourners in the El Dorado to be built, as hands necessary for the economy but not as persons welcome into the society. This was, and still is, the South African approach to race relations. Embodying this approach in their legislation, made within the framework of the South African jurisprudence of Roman-Dutch law (which they adopted), the Rhodesian settlers regarded the Rhodesian Africans as laborers who left their homes in the rural areas to seek employment in European zones, but then would return to their own permanent homes in the special areas, the reserves.

Thus, the Municipal Act of 1897 empowered municipalities to discriminate against Africans. They could determine where the Africans could live, where and when they could be during night and day, and what facilities they could generally have. In terms of this law, the Bulawayo municipality passed a regulation stating that no African could walk on a street pavement, and established a fine of not more than two pounds (about six dollars). To our knowledge, the first court case under this law was in 1934 when a convicted African was set free on appeal on the reasonable grounds that if he was allowed to go shopping in town, then he had to be permitted to use the pavement. Although rarely invoked, the law's very existence created resentment among Africans and, with other obnoxious measures, contributed in the end to the rise of nationalist opposition in the towns.

Another source of friction was the division of land. In staking out their gold claims and farms, the settlers apportioned to themselves some of the best lands. When they failed to find gold and other minerals in quantities large enough to rival those in Kimberley and in the Transvaal, the disappointed settlers switched, after 1900, to agriculture, stock raising and tobacco planting. As a result, many Africans, already living there for generations, found themselves "squatters" on legally sequestered European property.

The BSAC implemented land division by dividing the whole country into three categories: (1) land alienated to settlers; (2) land subject to alienation though temporarily occupied by Africans; and (3) land designated as native reserves or unalienated land. In 1914, settler area covered some 21,000,000 acres, while categories 2 and 3 totaled 70,000,000 acres. The company claimed the latter as its own property[5] to be dealt with—along with the Africans on it—as it saw fit. Since the BSAC charter had explicitly stated that the company was to pay careful attention to the interests of the Africans, especially in matters regarding the "holding, possession, transfer and disposition of lands," the British government became concerned in the first decade of this century and appointed a Natives Reserves Commission to study the matter.

In its interim report, the Commission of 1915 observed:

> The Matabele began to feel the pressure of European settlement within a very few months after the occupation. By the middle of 1894, practically the whole of the gold belt areas of Matabeleland had been alienated to companies or individuals, and although a large number of the farms granted were not at first actually occupied, it became necessary to consider the desirability of demarcating areas in other parts of the country which should be reserved from European occupation, and where the natives could live according to their own tribal system.[6]

Since most of the lands upon which the Africans had long resided were now alienated to the settlers, the Commission recommended that the only solution was to set aside special areas (reserves), distant from the Africans' original homes. These were to be the Shangani and the Gwaai Reserves. Others followed, so that in terms of area, the Africans at that time had a fairly large portion to occupy. But the change was too abrupt and too uprooting, and very few settled in the reserves. African resentment grew in Rhodesia over this high-handedness, just as it did in South Africa over the Land Act of 1913. The resentment was to unite the Africans in both countries in opposition to the land-hungry Boers and settlers. Together, they fought the issue in London, in the law courts and in political organizations.

The land problem and the ruthless implementation of the hut tax were a boon to the settlers. To avoid starvation, the

Africans were forced to seek employment in European areas, in the mines and on the farms. But compared with the demand, the available labor supply was a mere trickle; far more laborers were needed. So in 1901 the Legislative Council passed a law to allow for the importation of laborers from Asia, especially from what a Rhodesian, Frank Johnson, called "the one unlimited source of labour supply available in Asia viz: China."[7] Attractive though it was, the idea never gained much support in Rhodesia because South Africa had a disappointing experience with indentured Indian and Chinese laborers. In London, the chairman of the influential Royal Colonial Institute opposed the scheme because the industrious Chinese could become a competitive threat.[8]

The settlers felt that the best solution was to mobilize African labor. Following the 1895 initiative of the Rhodesian Chamber of Mines, the government organized in 1903 the Rhodesian Native Labor Bureau to recruit for the mines, farms and public services. The effectiveness of this measure in ensuring a steady supply of labor can be judged from the estimate of the South African Native Affairs Commission that in 1905 about 50 per cent of all males between fifteen and forty years of age were expected at any given time to be at work. Thus by 1921, when a census was taken, the following figures showing the distribution of labor appeared:

Agriculture:	52,542	Industries:	5,073
Mining:	44,005	Commerce:	4,621
Private households:	14,824	Independent artisans:	29

As to the quality of the labor, the Rhodesian Native Affairs Committee of Enquiry proudly quotes, as true of Rhodesia, the findings of the South African Native Affairs Commission of 1905, which said:

> The theory that the South African natives are hopelessly indolent may be dismissed as not being in accordance with the facts. Even the simple wants of the native population cannot be supplied without some degree of exertion. . . . The labour of tilling the soil, weeding, and reaping is shared, but is by no means exclusively performed by the native women; and the representation of the native living at his own village a lazy and luxurious life, supported by his wife or wives, is misleading.[9]

The Committee thus found Africans hard working, not lazy as Nurse Green had said of the Mashona.

To control the mobility of the African labor force, Jameson in 1895 introduced for adult males a system of passes which he copied from the Cape. How these worked is illustrated by this example given by the Committee of Enquiry:

> When a native changes his domicile from one district to another, he is provided with a pass which he presents to the official of his new district: he is then re-registered, surrendering the old registration certificate.[10]

These documents, clearly distinct from registration certificates and issued by special Pass Officers, applied (and still do) also to employment, residence and travel outside one's tribal district. In fact, without a pass no African could get a railway ticket. From the start, the restrictions caused resentment and hardship, which the Committee of Enquiry admitted:

> It is undeniable that at present very great hardship is imposed upon those who desire to observe the requirements of the law. For instance, it was shewn that a native might have to travel over 200 miles to get a pass to go to a few miles.[11]

Those who traveled without passes were arrested in large numbers until the government intervened and asked the Native Commissioners not to press charges in such cases. But even this relaxation of the law was found inadequate by the Committee, which said, "If it is clear that any portion of the law is regarded as oppressive, it would seem right to modify it or remove it from the Statute Book."[12] Considering the importance of pass controls to the settlers and the fact that this was a government committee, the suggestion was daring and revolutionary. If followed, the settlers feared that they would be flooded by natives from the congested and poor reserves, and the municipalities foresaw slums developing around the towns. It is small wonder, then, that this suggestion was shelved!

Nonetheless, there was a heavy influx of Africans into the urban areas—under prodding from the settlers. The more Africans who came, the lower their wages would be. Reports of forced labor were made to the British government by the Resident Commissioners in 1897 and 1902. As a result, the Africans found themselves congested near the towns in residential areas called locations. The Committee of Enquiry regarded conditions there as most unsatisfactory: "There is . . . very little semblance of home life in any location . . . and we think this accounts for a good deal of the disorder and immorality which is reported to be prevalent in them. Forms of recreation are few, other than gambling and drinking."[13] The immorality mentioned here is prostitution, of which the Committee went on to say that "prior to our rule prostitution was practically unknown amongst natives, as the punishment was so severe." As for drinking, the Committee reported that the "*sale* of beer is contrary to all native traditions, and is largely the cause of moral decline."[14] But while contradicting Nurse Green (who found vice among the Mashona) and pointing out the cause of the whole trouble—occupation by the settlers—the Committee did not advocate the logical solution: namely, ending the occupation so that tribal discipline should return. Instead, it recommended, among other things, that there be set up improved dwellings and refreshment houses, as had been successfully done by the city of Durban in South Africa.

There are a number of points in the Committee report which do credit to the integrity and objectivity of its members. Yet one always discerns the basic assumption that the settlers have a superior way of life which has to be maintained and thus African education had to be geared to the settler's interests. As in most areas in Africa, the education of the indigenous population was undertaken by missionaries, since the government saw no immediate gain from such a venture. When the settlers in Rhodesia did, the Administration passed an ordinance in 1903 which gave grants to native schools on condition that they systematically taught industrial work and farming for at least two hours a day during the school year. Although the missionaries had found it difficult to implement this law because they had few qualified teachers, the public was generally satisfied with the missionaries' work. As a result, the Education Committee of 1908, appointed to inquire into and report on the laws and educational system in the country, deliberately excluded African education from its work because there was no "a priori evidence showing that there was dissatisfaction with the provisions made by the Ordinance for native education."[15] Nor did it, for the same reason, deal with the education of the "large and growing number of half-caste children."[16]

The first signs of concern among the settlers appeared about 1910, when some Africans who had received training in South Africa began to question certain aspects of the settler regime. The Committee of Enquiry of 1910–1911 reported that some settlers preferred to keep the African as a "raw untutored menial, but there was gratifying proof in plenty of the realisation that in this country our own development is so clearly interwoven with that of the native that it is vital for our own interests, as well as for his, that he be mentally raised and encouraged to improve himself."[17] In the Committee's opinion, the African could best improve himself through education that equally stressed the religious, literary and industrial aspects of life. The Committee found religion important, not because of its intrinsic worth as a force binding man to his Creator, but because it could be used to control the African. Since primitive superstition was so strong a force controlling the actions of Africans, the Committee thought it necessary "for our own sakes . . . to replace that control by some other restraining influence."[18] In other words, religion was a useful tool to enable the settler to keep the African in his place.

But religion had to be subject to settler control—or be suspect. This was the case with the Ethiopian Movement, a Christian sectarian movement that established a separate black man's church and sought to attract Africans from the white-dominated churches which treated them as outsiders. The Committee took note of the movement, but decided, incorrectly, that it was not a threat, since South African blacks dominated it and Rhodesian blacks were supposedly suspicious of such foreigners. While dismissing the danger of the Ethiopian Movement, the Committee warned that "any exponents of its teachings in the Territory be carefully watched."[19]

In other words, the Committee was recommending that any religious sect over which the settlers had no control needed watching. As the rise of African nationalism was to show, the watching proved inadequate.

Interestingly enough, the Committee felt compelled to deal with higher education as well. Since the country did not have facilities for completion of high school, the Committee was alarmed that the student might even go outside the country which was acceptable, South Africa. "This," they warned, "we must set ourselves to obviate. When he returns, he is filled with a spirit of unrest and dissatisfaction with his surroundings and is imbued with ideas which, if communicated to the people amongst whom he settles, may become a source of danger to their peace and quiet."[20] Clearly the settlers saw in education a danger to the status quo. Small wonder, then, that the budget for African education in Rhodesia has always been very low.

In 1920, the Report on the Suggested Industrial Development of Natives was compiled by the Cambridge University graduate Herbert Keigwin, who had acted as secretary to the Native Affairs Committee of Enquiry of 1910–1911. He epitomized the inclination to gear African education to the economic needs of the settlers. While expressing "grateful recognition of the good work" done by the missionaries, Native Commissioner Keigwin said: "Their zeal for the spiritual and the literary has been too little tempered with regard for the material and industrial. The result has often been that the avenue of advancement has been very largely that of the mental rather than the material."[21] In more mundane terms, he charged that mission schools were not training Africans in keeping with the material or economic needs of the country.

He recommended that African education deal more with "industries that lend themselves to primitive hand methods." Such a policy, he pointed out, was being successfully applied by the Belgians in the Congo with the aim of raising the whole mass of the African population rather than a few individuals. With the whole mass equally educated, he argued, "The educated agitator will not have the same ignorant populace to work upon, and his inflammatory doctrines will have less chance of success. Racial friction will be less likely to occur."[22] His solution was that the African should start at the very bottom of industrial development, in the simplest home industries—food production, pottery, carpentry, smithing and basketmaking.

Keigwin shows three features of the settler mind: first of all, that education can breed agitators who urge their fellow Africans to oppose the settlers; and second, that every African should be treated as a child who has to advance step by step under the watchful eye and stern supervision of the parent from Europe or South Africa. Keigwin was not tilting at imaginary windmills; there were already Africans who were questioning the basis of settler rule—their claim to the land. The third feature is the settler conviction that for the African economic or material development should come before politics.

This heavy emphasis on the material side of life must be seen in the context of the company's activities from the beginning of the occupation. As a financial corporation, it was concerned with making a profit. But first it had to invest tons of money into the infrastructure: telegraphs, roads and railways to facilitate the transportation of heavy mining and farming equipment from South Africa and England. As a result of this investment, the company did not produce any dividends until years later in 1907. In the meantime, however, it had to gear all the available resources, both human and material, toward making a success of the venture it had begun. Labor mobility had to be controlled, and the education of the African, whose labor was the basis of the economic fabric, had to fall into line because, said Keigwin, "frankly we want his co-operation in building up the prosperity of the State as a whole."

In this era when the company strove to turn a profit and to govern the country according to South African precepts, the seeds of African nationalism were sown. Meanwhile, by the time Cecil Rhodes died in Cape Town in 1902, hopes of amicable relations between the Boers and the British had been shattered in the Anglo-Boer War (1899–1902). A colorful character, and a man of action popular with the settlers for protecting their interests from both the British government and the company, Rhodes' last words were, "So much to do, so little done." He left behind his famous scholarships (which have yet to include a Rhodesian African) and his dream for the white settlers. In the twenty years after his death, that dream materialized at least in the favored position of the white settlers and the company, the BSAC. It could be said of the period leading up to the emergence of Rhodesia as a self-governing colony in 1923 that the British Crown had reigned but the company ruled.

CHAPTER FOUR

THE END OF COMPANY RULE

With the end of World War I, the African sun began to set rapidly upon the rule of the British South Africa Company over Rhodesia. This was not surprising, for it had been evident from the very start of the occupation that the settlers would not tolerate permanent government by a commercial body. The love of freedom, strong among both the Boers and the Britons, was bound to lead to demands for self-government.

As these demands gained momentum, one point stood out starkly and clearly: though the settlers favored the South African approach toward the "native problem," they did not want to be incorporated into South Africa. Instead, on the whole, they championed the development of a distinct Rhodesian nation—unwavering in its loyalty to the Crown, even though forged out of the disparate elements of Boer and Briton.

From the start of the company's rule, the settlers disapproved, on principle, of being ruled by a commercial organization. They reasoned that the private interests of the shareholders necessarily must outweigh the public ones. Despite repeated and spirited attempts, the company could not stem the tide of discontent. As early as 1901, a candidate stood unsuccessfully for election to the Legislative Council on a ticket supporting independence from the company. In 1902, Charles Coghlan, a Bulawayo lawyer of Irish descent and educated at the high-ranking Jesuit college of St. Aidan's in South Africa, began denouncing the double role of the company as repugnant to anyone of British stock.

What particularly irked the settlers was their failure to quickly find the rich and long-promised gold deposits. Furthermore, in their grim struggle to eke out an existence, they had to pay taxes to the company, which acted both as ruler on behalf of the Crown and as a moneymaking enterprise with primary responsibility to its shareholders. The situation was unacceptable but tolerable so long as the company made no profit; the company ruled with its majority of members in the Legislative Council. When the company began to balance its books in 1907 and to show a profit, the situation became intolerable. The company ploughed the profits back into its public and commercial activities so that money raised through taxation thus served a double purpose: it not only paid for government but also provided revenue for the company. This development infuriated the settlers, and found eloquent expression in the writings of the first lady to be elected to parliament in any of Britain's colonies, Mrs. Ethel Tawse Jollie.[1]

The immediate upshot was that the settlers demanded majority representation in the Legislative Council. In 1911, they were assigned seven elected members to the company's five; by 1914, they had twelve, and the company still five. One of their members was elected on the ticket of self-government. Not wishing to interfere unduly and further aggravate matters, the British government allowed the settlers a free hand in making laws, provided these did not violate the Constitution. As a result, Rhodesia could deal with Africans almost at will.

With the Privy Council deciding against it in 1918, the company lost the economic motivation to govern, since this now entailed immense liabilities. By then, the country was rather prosperous; automobiles, motorcycles and radios were beginning to appear as the mines and the farms increasingly paid their way. Political debate was very lively on the issue of whether Rhodesia was to be incorporated as a province of the Union of South Africa. The majority of settlers opposed such a step and Dr. Jameson, the former Administrator, energetically put forth their viewpoint in a fiery speech. Speaking as a physician, he painted a frightening picture: "What is going to happen to this young, vigorous Rhodesian child when it gets into the bed of that large and corpulent mother, the Union? What always happens? In this case at all events all your aspirations are going to be killed, and at the inquest next morning, the verdict will be 'overlaid by the Union.' "[2]

In the elections of March, 1920, all but one of the elected candidates won on the ticket of self-rule, the odd man out being R. A. Fletcher, who supported the extension of the company's rule. The Legislative Council then asked Lord Milner, now the Colonial Secretary, for immediate self-government. Because his recommendation that another election be held on this issue was rejected by his colleagues in the British Cabinet, he resigned, and was succeeded in 1921 by Winston Churchill. The latter appointed a commission (the Buxton Commission) to investigate the issue of Rhodesian self-government. While recommending self-government, the Commission added that the Africans should be placed under the High Commissioner to South Africa, who at the same time was Governor-General to the Union. This recommendation meant that the Africans were to be ruled by the South African government. Naturally, the settlers were indignant, for the suggestion indicated mistrust in their ability to hold a trusteeship over the "natives." "Do they [the Buxton Commission] suppose that we live in the jungle?" asked Charles Coghlan, the settler leader.

Churchill's reply in 1921 was to insist to a settler delegation in London that his friend, the Prime Minister of South Africa, General Smuts, be given a chance to bid for incorporating Rhodesia. To the company, Smuts offered as compensation more than the British government (five million pounds to two million). To the settlers he dangled the prospect of loans for irrigation schemes, land settlement and general development, apart from ten seats in the South African Parliament, four in the Senate, a Provincial Council of twenty members, and for Coghlan a Cabinet post. But the offer was not tempting enough; neither was Smuts' visit to Salisbury, ostensibly to open an agricultural and a cattle show, even though aided by some local Boer propaganda.

In a referendum held on October 27, 1922, after three months of campaigning on responsible government or joining the Union, the result was: 8,774 votes for responsible government, and 5,989 for Union, a majority of 2,785 out of 14,763 votes cast. All the electoral districts, except one at Marandellas, favored responsible government. General Smuts and Churchill were disappointed at the outcome; but a number of factors seemingly played a decisive role. First of all, merger with the Union would have meant the end of the distinct British character of Rhodesia, since in the Union the Boers formed the majority and insisted that their language, Afrikaans, be accorded equal status with English, whereas in Rhodesia, Afrikaans was not even used in the schools. Secondly, the scale of taxation in Rhodesia was the lowest in the whole British Empire, and for the struggling settlers to opt for the Union would have meant higher taxes. Also, incorporation would siphon off African workers to the Union, which paid higher wages. For their part, the European workers feared General Smuts, who had just ruthlessly put down a strike by European miners in Johannesburg by using troops and guns.

The rejection of South Africa by the settlers did not, however, signify a change in Rhodesia's official attitude toward the African. Native policy continued to follow the South African pattern.

On October 1, 1923, Rhodesia with her 35,000 settlers emerged with a baffling constitutional status, that of a self-governing colony. It has never been clear to Africans in Rhodesia and in the rest of the continent how a territory can be self-governing and still be a colony. On the face of it, Rhodesia has the trappings of self-rule familiar within the British Commonwealth. Until 1964, her Prime Minister was always invited to the conference of Commonwealth Premiers. Moreover, Rhodesia like all other dominions was administered from 1923 by Britain through the Commonwealth Relations Office, not the Colonial Office. Though her foreign relations were under the control of the British government, this was only technically the case. Later events in the 1960's were to support the contention of some Africans that the settlers had been conducting their own foreign policy all along, with London merely acquiescing after the deed. But as long as successive British governments, both Conservative and Labour, maintained in Parliament and at the United Nations that they held the final power, the Africans insisted that she exercise it on behalf of their brothers. Britain's failure to do so is regarded as a violation of the unequivocal 1923 guarantee for Africans' rights—which the settlers are now violating with impunity.

The baffling constitutional position of Rhodesia, culminating in the 1965 Unilateral Declaration of Independence by Mr. Ian Smith and other acts of settler defiance, demonstrates the point made by Professor Holleman of Leiden University: " . . . despite explicit regulations and directives constitutionally provided for by the distant mother-country, it is the local factors and insights which in the first place and to a great extent determine the development of local events."[3]

What, then, was the position of the Africans under the 1923 Constitution? First of all, as in 1898, Britain reserved to herself the right to veto laws discriminating against Africans. This was intended as a safeguard for their interests, although, as Miss Margery Perham has pointed out, in the entire course of Rhodesian history Britain "failed to use it to prevent the increasing gap between white privilege and economic power, and African subordination."[4] Secondly, Britain handed back to the settlers control over the armed forces, which could be used without the authorization of the Crown. This concession was to have very serious consequences, leaving Rhodesia virtually free to do as she liked at home. She became all the more convinced of her ability to defend herself against any internal uprising and felt that she could even stand up against invaders. Indeed, the very possession of an army seemed to her a guarantee that Britain would never dare use troops against the settlers.

The changeover did not bring about a new political status for the Africans. Unlike South Africa which started separate political representation for the Africans, Rhodesia kept the Cape Colony system of permitting a minority of Africans to be on the common voters' roll. Until 1951 the voting qualifications for all Rhodesians, black and white, were the same—namely, the possession of property with an annual value of £150 or a yearly income of £100. Both were accompanied by a simple test in English. In 1951 the Rhodesian government tried to provide for separate representation, but soon dropped the scheme largely because of British opposition. Instead, it was permitted to raise the financial qualifications so high that very few Africans managed to qualify.

As an initial act the self-governing colony regulated permanently the division of the land among the Europeans and the Africans. For the settlers, this was a logical step, since they viewed their interests as separate from those of the indigenous population. The prevailing feeling was that the European was safest with the African securely rooted to his tribal life in the reserves, where he presented the least threat to settler rule. Consequently, missionaries who entered the reserves to spread the Gospel or to found schools aroused much suspicion, and even anger. The reason is that some of the Africans who had gone through mission schools (the so-called mission boys) did not behave like their docile fellows in the reserves. Hence, the preference in both Rhodesia and South Africa for the "unspoiled native" rather than the partly educated and stubborn one. The trouble with the latter—as Dr. Verwoerd was to say before the South African Senate in June 1954—was that he was the product of an educational system which "misled him by showing him the green pastures of European society in which he is not allowed to graze." Indirectly, then, the missionaries were regarded as subversives, a threat to the maintenance of white rule. The mission schools had, therefore, to be closely watched, just as the land issue had to be settled quickly and permanently. An additional reason for doing so was that agriculture was becoming the main occupation and the Africans were also living off it; land became a burning political issue.

The debates over land took on a rather bitter note because the 1898 Constitution had given Africans the right to acquire and dispose of land in the same way as Europeans. In practice, however, very few ever used this right, since the Native Commissioners discouraged them. Still, its very existence gave rise to grave concern among the settlers lest in the future the Africans should exercise it to secure more land for their fast-growing numbers. Socially, the settlers dreaded the prospect of having these uncivilized people as neighbors. To make things worse, the Africans were supposedly poor farmers; the settlers feared that the agricultural habits of the Africans would soon make a desert out of otherwise good soil and their cattle would ravage the stock of the settlers and cause hybridization.

The fears about African acquisition of land were not altogether baseless, for by 1925 a few Africans were using their constitutional right to buy land anywhere in the country, and now owned some 45,000 acres. Foreseeing friction, the Chief Native Commissioner, Herbert J. Taylor, recommended that special areas be set aside near the reserves for purchase by Africans only.[5] Alarmed, the 1921 delegation to London urged Churchill to act on this recommendation. He refused, but added that if impartial study of the problem showed the need for new legislation, then the British government would consider the matter. Following this suggestion, the Rhodesian government in 1925 set up the Morris Carter Commission. Its conclusions, similar to Taylor's, are embodied in the Land Apportionment Act of 1930 (amended in 1941), which has been called the "Magna Carta of the Europeans" because it is one of the pillars of the Rhodesian social and racial structure. This law divided the whole country into native areas, European areas and unallocated lands, with the Africans getting about 33 per cent, the Europeans some 50 per cent (including the urban areas), and the rest remaining unallocated. To those Africans living (or "squatting," to use the local word) on European lands, the law gave six years' notice to quit and return to the reserves or buy land in their own Native Purchase Areas. This provision is in full keeping with the Stallard Commission of South Africa, which in 1922 had said that the sole reason for the African's presence in European areas is that he should "minister to the needs of the white man and should depart therefrom when he ceases to so minister."

While it is true that one of the worthwhile aims of this law was to save the Africans from further exploitation by land-hungry non-Africans, it nevertheless engendered much ill-feeling and added to the Africans' opposition to the land policies of the settlers. Rural Africans opposed it because it restricted their growing multitudes to poor soil. Urban Africans resented it because it ordained that in the towns they could not own property or occupy premises. Thus the law has had to be amended to enable an African barrister, Mr. H. Chitepo, to occupy the same building as his colleagues and also to allow African students to live on the site of the University College in Salisbury. Both amendments were strenuously but vainly opposed by the Segregation Society, founded in 1954.

As a further result of this law, locations, which the Committee of Enquiry of 1910–1911 found to be horrible, became worse in the cities. There was overcrowding, little privacy, hardly any accommodation for the married men—all because these urban workers were regarded as temporary sojourners. But it must be said, though not in justification of the grim conditions in the locations, that a good number of Africans were from Northern Rhodesia (now Zambia), Nyasaland (now Malawi), and Mozambique and were planning to return home.

To consolidate land division, the government introduced in 1951 the much-disputed Land Husbandry Act. It purports to revolutionize African agriculture by promoting good farming methods, like continuous cultivation of the soil and destocking of cattle, and by encouraging individual ownership of land. But this law must be seen within the context of African traditional life. As a result of the 1930 Land Apportionment Act, much of the African land was parceled out among families. These small holdings were in turn subdivided among children when they married as families grew larger. The result was that the available land was reduced in size to below arable proportions. Some families became practically landless.

The Land Husbandry Act, which was passed to combat this problem, has met with vehement criticism. Why? Some agricultural experts consider it a bad measure because it aims at continuous cultivation on soils which are unsuited for it, and thereby perpetuates soil erosion in the reserves. The African angle can be gauged from the famous statement by Mr. George Nyandoro, Secretary-General of the Rhodesian African National Congress (now banned but replaced by ZAPU) that "the Land Husbandry Act has been the best recruiter Congress ever had."

By encouraging individual ownership, the act violated the spirit of communal ownership and assistance, and deprived the chiefs of their power over the people to whom traditionally they allot land and in exchange get loyalty. Moreover, destocking means the reduction of the African's most highly prized possession, cattle, which is a measure of his wealth and status. Finally, as a former agricultural officer in Rhodesia, Ken Brown, has shown,[6] when feeling the harsh effects of this law, the Africans in the reserves can with bitterness (and, no doubt, envy) look across the border at the European farmlands, mostly undeveloped, often of better quality but often unused.

The effect of the two major land laws (plus earlier land policies) was to unite the Africans in the towns and in the reserves against the settlers. Both laws brought closer together the chiefs and their subjects, the town dwellers and the peasants, the educated and the illiterate, for their struggle was one. Nyandoro's statement is, therefore, no exaggeration.

The opposition from the chiefs throws an interesting light

on their status under the rule of the settlers. In traditional African society, the chief is the leader and representative of his people. Land belongs to the people as a whole, with the chief merely allotting it to individual families and to visitors wishing to settle. By justly distributing it and seeing to its proper upkeep, he wins the loyalty and respect of his people. The coming of the white settlers shattered this tribal order. The land was taken away; the chiefs became salaried officials, appointed or recognized by the settler administration. Their duty was to cooperate with the local Native Commissioner and to help collect taxes and to arrest transgressors of the law. This role was bound to alienate them from their followers, to whom they appeared as "sell-outs." They lost the respect of their people, for a chief without land under his jurisdiction is nothing. A chief who takes the side of the oppressor against his own people is himself an enemy. With no choice in the matter, they were (and still are) in a compromising position. Some confronted their dilemma by opposing the settlers and joining hands with the urban Africans; others decided to throw in their lot with the settlers. Judgment has already long been passed on the latter by their followers. Writing in the twenties, Charles Bullock observed: "Today you may see Natives passing their Chiefs with little or no formal salutation. When reproved, they may say: 'Where is the land?' That is to say: 'The Whites are now owners of the land. Why should we salute a landless man?' "[7]

Under Rhodesia's new status the African industrial worker was also victimized. The steady growth of the colony's industrial resources was coupled with the enticing of European immigrants after the First World War. The ensuing competition between black and white workers, whether skilled or not, forced the government to legalize the color bar already existing in the industrial sector whereby African laborers were paid less than their European counterparts. The issue was of immense political import to future race relations. The government's solution was the Industrial Conciliation Act of 1934 which established Industrial Councils, machinery for settling disputes. The act stipulated that agreements reached between employers and employees were to be binding for the whole industry in question, and that employers were to be forbidden to employ skilled labor at wage rates lower than those fixed by agreement. This was a subterfuge which had the effect of freezing the African in unskilled jobs.

The cruel device was exclusion of African workers from the term "employee." Instead, they were classified as native laborers and therefore not eligible for any job classified as skilled. All that was required for a job to become skilled was an agreement negotiated in any single company within an industry; the agreement automatically applied to all other companies in the same industry. To get around this legal requirement, an employer could place an African in a skilled job if he listed it as unskilled and paid the African laborer's pay.

He could do this legally—but not in the political atmosphere that prevailed. He would be placed under severe pressure from fellow employers, government officials, politicians and, most of all, white skilled workers in his company. The special interest of white workers called for higher wages, while the political policy of the regime called for encouraging immigration of white workers with the lure of high wages.

Another African disability under this law was that the Industrial Councils were given the power to determine the conditions of apprenticeship. Since by definition they could not be employees, training in modern industrial skills was thus impossible for the Africans. Since the depression of the 1930's this law has been a convenient tool for institutionalizing job reservation on racial grounds. As Prime Minister Godfrey Huggins pointed out with characteristic candor, the Africans were excluded because they were a threat to "the economic structure of the white race," not because they lacked the innate capacity to learn, as is implied by Native Commissioner Keigwin's recommendation in 1920 that they be taught simple and primitive skills.

Their exclusion led to an artificial scarcity of skilled labor which has had to be filled by importing skilled European labor at high inducement wages. Consequently, the white workers have come to occupy a privileged position, the abolition of which may well bring down their inflated wages. The very idea frightens them. As Colin Leys says, "European wage-earners resist any measure which is liable to reduce it [their high wage level], and in this they are generally supported by the rest of the European community, since the existing situation appears to guarantee a continued high standard of living to their children."[8]

An additional guarantee lies in keeping feeble and powerless the African labor unions. In the 1920's the government tried, but failed, to discourage the African-run Industrial and Commercial Workers' Union of South Africa (ICU) from entering Rhodesia to organize unions. Before 1960, Africans could not belong to recognized labor unions, which meant those run by Europeans. Even after this time, trade union activity by Africans has been hampered by all sorts of restrictions.

These restrictions and other disabilities have served to stoke the cinders of the simmering conflict between the settlers and the Africans. All that was needed now was organizations that would channel African grievances, a leadership that would be articulate and nationalist. The lines of battle were clearly drawn, for as the settler spokesman, Mrs. Jollie, admiringly noted of Rhodesia, "Climatically and politically it is a white man's country: socially it is a white aristocracy with a black proletariat."[9] Of such divisions are conflicts born; on such divisions do they feed.

CHAPTER FIVE

THE RISE OF AFRICAN NATIONALISM

What is African nationalism? It is a sociopolitical phenomenon hard to pin down. Certainly, the origins are not the same as for European nationalism, which developed among a people with a range of common characteristics embracing religion, language, history, culture. In Europe growing awareness of these features almost invariably led to war in order to enshrine them in a political entity—the state. In Africa, the process of nationalism ran a different course. The feeling and consciousness of oneness grew out of resentment against alien rule, however well-meaning.

The leading African nationalists preferred self-government

even to good government as epitomized in these oft-quoted statements: "We prefer self-government with danger to servitude with tranquility" (Nkrumah). "We prefer poverty in freedom to riches in slavery" (Sekou Touré). In the political challenge to colonial rule, most of the disparate, and sometimes warring, ethnic units submerged their differences for the sake of achieving the common goal of independence. Thus in Africa, the reverse of European nationalism seemed to be taking place: there was little or no war before unity in the state. Nationalism in Africa was largely a movement against a common enemy: the colonizer. It was not characterized by emergence of groups or tribes imposing their way of life on neighbors.

For these reasons, Lord Hailey prefers the term Africanism to nationalism. However, I have reserved the term Africanism for Pan-Africanism, that movement which transcends ethnic and politicolegal boundaries and seeks to unite the entire continent of Africa. Nationalism remains appropriate because this term shows contact with Europe in two respects. First of all, far from rejecting Europe and all her pomp, the Africans increasingly sought, during and after the struggle, to be Westernized, to graft on to their own social fabric the spirit, technological orientation and values of Europe. This is inevitable since the African leaders have learned and developed their public and professional styles in European schools in Africa or Europe itself. The lessons they have learned are the key to participation in the life of the international community as well, whether this is within or outside the African continent. Secondly, the recent power struggles in African states—some bloodless, others gory and grisly—seem to presage the start of what can be called the European nationalist process of one group trying to dominate others. It would seem that the unity of the colonial struggle was only a temporary marriage of convenience. Consequently the nationalisms of Europe and Africa emerge as similar phenomena in terms of aims and outcomes, though pursued and developed in different sequences.

In Rhodesia the seeds of African nationalism were planted in the very land that the settlers seized from the Africans. Without land, the African was robbed of his pride, his economic heritage, his family's rootedness in the soil of his forefathers. Like Cain, Africans became fugitives and vagabonds. The taking of their land was provocation, the white man the provoker.

The first to rise were the Mandebele, though their proud, militaristic tribal armies were defeated in 1893 and again in 1896, even after joining forces with the Mashona in 1897. The latter uprising marked the end of tribal resistance and the beginning of supertribal or nationalist opposition. With King Lobengula's death, the kingship, which was the pivot of the Mandebele's identity, was abolished by the settlers to prevent future trouble. African religion then provided the driving force.

But a flashback is necessary to set the role of religion in perspective. After conquering the Barozwi in the 1830's, the Mandebele, to keep the peace, left untouched and then assimilated the religion of the Barozwi, which dated back to the Makaranga and the Monomotapa era.[1] This religion centered on the high god called the Mlimu or Mwari. Even King Lobengula paid homage to this awesome deity at the latter's headquarters in the Matopo Hills. So also did the ordinary people who betook themselves to the Mlimu for advice and for help in propitiating other gods. With the abolition of the kingship by the settlers, the high priest of this religion superseded the Mandebele kings, and the Mlimu-Mwari religion became the rallying point necessary for any uprising, since it had deep roots in both Mashonaland and Matabeleland. Thus in the 1893 and 1896–97 uprisings the religious motive power was personified in a priest called Mkwati. After the 1893 failure, which was followed by the settler introduction of land division and the pass laws, Mkwati urged first the Mandebele, then the Mashona, to drive out the white men, the source of all their travails. But the Mlimu was no match for the Maxim guns, and the African struggle failed. Mkwati himself met a dreadful death. Ranger quotes a participant in the uprising, Mhlope, as saying that the Mashona "killed him in a curious way. They cut him up into pieces while he was alive with choppers. They said that if he was the man sent by the Mlimu, they had better make sure he could not come to life again and make more trouble."[2]

In 1896, the struggle became Pan-African, though ethnic. The Scottish missionary Joseph Booth went to Natal in South Africa to propagate his scheme of an African Christian Union to help the Africans regain their dignity. There he found among the Zulu "a suspicion of the white man which had reached the point of bitterness and hatred"[3] because of the white man's broken promises. Some 120 Zulus told him that they had no faith any more "in the blood-stained white men, who had slain thousands of Zulus and their Matabele relations."[4] This loss of confidence spurred the growth in South Africa of the Ethiopian Movement, which spread to Rhodesia in the 1920's.

After the uprisings in Rhodesia, two short-lived tribal acts of defiance were put down. In his annual reports, Mr. W. S. Taberer, the Chief Native Commissioner for Mashonaland, wrote of Chief Mapondera, who refused to levy the settlers' taxes on his people. In defiance, he slipped across the border to Mozambique, and returned with a force to fight the government police. Though defeated, he escaped arrest[5] and continued to harass them. But lacking widespread support, his resistance petered out. A similar fate befell the defiance of Chief Kunzwi-Nyandoro.[6] Their main weakness was lack of religious inspiration on which the traditional leadership in Mashonaland largely depended.

Among the Mandebele, on the other hand, a modern approach emerged among their traditional rulers. After defeating the Mandebele in 1893, Rhodes had two sons of King Lobengula, Njube and Nguboyena, educated in the Cape Province, South Africa, at the leading college for Africans, Lovedale College,[7] which received a grant from the Rhodesian government. Members of the Mandebele aristocracy also studied at this college or at another one called Tiger Kloof, near Vryburg in the northern Cape.[8] Nguboyena, a brilliant student, intended to study law but was dissuaded from doing so by the Secretary of the British South Africa Company, who told him to "take the word of those wiser and more experienced than himself that it could not be." "In the event," remarks Ranger, "Nguboyena became the first victim of the transition from one world to another; withdrew from his Law course, and relapsed into sullen insanity under guard in Cape Town."[9]

Thus a large section of the Mandebele leadership was in touch with modern developments. Much to the disappointment of the Administration which thought that Lobengula's death marked the end of the monarchy, a large following wanted the kingship revived. The illiterate and the emerging group of clerks, schoolteachers and preachers joined forces for this purpose. In their work, they were supported by their ethnic brethren in South Africa—the Nguni, the Zulus and the Xhosas, who had remained behind when they left in the 1830's under Mzilikazi and Zwangendaba. Later, the opening of gold and diamond mines in South Africa and the absence of good schools in Rhodesia drew many Mandebele to South Africa. As a result, they were again in close touch with their old kith and kin with whom they share a rather similar language and culture.[10] Another ethnic tie existed through the Fingo people of Nguni stock who settled in Rhodesia in the late 1890's, and were to play an important role in the political modernization of the Mandebele.

The issue which cemented these ties was land. As the company and the settlers acquired more and more land, the Mandebele's share drastically decreased. They became restless and shocked the government by rallying round one of King Lobengula's sons, Nyamanda. The government was surprised because at Njube's death in Grahamstown in the Cape in 1910, the Chief Native Commissioner for Matabeleland had confidently predicted that this marked the end of the line of succession to the throne.[11] With equal confidence, another commissioner reported that since Nyamanda had been born before Lobengula had been crowned king, he could not assume the tribal leadership. Besides, he reported, only a few people were interested in his claims. In the commissioner's judgment, the rest were "either entirely indifferent or actively opposed to an appointment, which, to their minds, threatens the peace and security of the present regime [the settlers]

. . ." because twenty-five years of "our rule has individualized the bulk of the Matabele to such a degree as to make them suspicious of the restraints of tribalism."[12] Both commissioners were proved completely out of touch with the feelings of their charges.

The demand for more land forced Nyamanda into prominence. Himself evicted from the Insiza area, he began airing his grievances and those of his people to government officials. One quotes him as saying that "being landless and at the mercy of any purchaser of land was a difficult position and a bitter pill for a man of his standing to swallow and that he felt that the Government had no sympathy or regard for his difficulties or troubles."[13] On behalf of his people he then demanded the creation of a Ndebele "National Home" where the Mandebele could be safe from harassing land-seekers.

The principal sources of support which Nyamanda had from among modern Africans in his bid for the National Home were the educatd Mandebele, clerks, teachers and preachers; prominent leaders of the Ethiopian Movement in both Rhodesia and South Africa; the Fingo people; African lawyers from Johannesburg; and the African National Congress of South Africa (ANC), a political organization founded in 1912 by Africans in South Africa to unite the various tribes in their fight against the Boers and the Britons.

The concern shown in 1896 by the Nguni people for the welfare of their brethren in Rhodesia increased over the years. In 1914, when the Privy Council began hearing the case on ownership of land, an ANC delegation and some missionaries presented a joint petition setting forth the claims of the Rhodesian Africans. Interestingly enough, this delegation had gone to London to protest against the Native Land Act of

1913, which, in the apt phrase of a contemporary African observer, Sol Plaatje, made the African "a pariah in the land of his birth"—what the Land Apportionment Act would do to his counterpart in Rhodesia. The delegation consisted of John L. Dube (President), Walter B. Rubusana, Sol T. Plaatje, Saul Msane and Thomas Mapikela. On his return from England, Dube intended to make "enquiries among the natives of Southern Rhodesia in order to ascertain whether any of them wish to proffer a claim to the unalienated land on behalf of the natives in their collective or tribal capacity, or even to ascertain whether any of the natives, who from their position as 'Indunas' of the late Lobengula or otherwise, can be persuaded to take such action."[14] Fearing racial disturbances, the Rhodesian government refused to let him into the country, but this did not bury the issue.

In 1918, the Fingos, who for some fourteen years had been unsuccessfully trying to buy land, asked a Johannesburg lawyer, Advocate Alfred Mangena, to help them. Since they and Nyamanda had similar interests and problems on the land issue, they asked him to offer legal aid to Nyamanda as well. The latter was very enthusiastic, but the settlers were alarmed and deported Mangena before he could formulate a strategy. Undaunted, he handed the case over to another lawyer, Richard W. Msimang, and seems to have encouraged the Ethiopian Movement of South Africa to take a keen interest in Nyamanda's problem. Strong in the south, but still weak in Rhodesia, its leaders were known to Nyamanda. One prominent figure in the South African section of the Movement was the Reverend Henry R. Ngcayiya, who at the same time was National Chaplain of the ANC. When discussions with Nyamanda and the Fingos led to a decision that another petition be sent to the British government, Ngcayiya in 1919 joined another ANC delegation destined for Versailles and London. Their efforts for both South Africa and Rhodesia were in vain. As Mary Benson says, ". . . they had a good press and the British people were friendly; a splendid banquet was put on for their entertainment, but they were arguing a hopeless case."[15]

Thereafter, Nyamanda and his supporters became convinced that it was futile to send delegations to the British government. Ranger quotes Abraham Twala as saying: "Experience has taught us that our salvation does not lie in Downing Street. I strongly advise our native fledglings in Southern Rhodesia, indulging in politics, to find out and make their friends in Southern Rhodesia. When this has been done we shall see what the harvest shall be."[16] Henceforth, efforts were to be focused on organizing in Rhodesia in order to exert as much pressure as possible on the home government. Thus in 1920 Nyamanda's colleagues set up the Rhodesian Bantu Voters' Association and the Southern Rhodesia Native Welfare Association. Both enjoyed the active support of the Mandebele aristocracy and their educated fellowmen in Rhodesia and in South Africa. Meanwhile the Rhodesian Native Association appeared in Mashonaland in 1920; its concern was the lot of the farmers and rural Mashona. All these organizations were modeled on others existing in South Africa. For example, the Voters' Association had close ties with the Bantu Vigilance Association of South Africa. Like the latter, it held among other things that "Work shall be effected by constitutional resolutions and peaceful propaganda and by consulting the Native Affairs Department, MPs and Missionaries."[17] J. van Velsen rightly describes these associations as follows:

These early societies tended to be run by and appeal to the new African elite who were greatly concerned to gain from the whites social recognition as "advanced natives" in contrast to the "uneducated masses." The aims and attitudes of these early associations clearly imply that they were resigned to white rule and had committed themselves to many aspects of a new, European modelled way of life. It is therefore not surprising that official white opinion at the time should refer to them as "reputable" organizations.[18]

Judged in terms of their goals, these associations achieved very little. There was far too wide a difference between their interests and those of the settlers and their government. The latter were heavily influenced by South Africa, making "inevitable the transplanting of the traditional authoritarian-paternalistic white attitude toward their African fellow citizens on virtually every level of the relations between black and white."[19] Nonetheless, these associations created among Africans a greater awareness of their common plight. Out of this awareness grew the nationalist sentiment.

More important and durable than these early associations was the African National Congress of Southern Rhodesia (ANCR), although its first attempt to organize in 1919 had been unsuccessful. A Rhodesian clergyman living in Johannesburg, P. S. Ngwenya, issued a manifesto, urging all black Rhodesians to send money and delegates to Johannesburg, the headquarters of the organization:

> From 1893 to 1919 the Government has been bad towards the brown man of Rhodesia. . . . It is good that you should contribute money and ask others to do so, money being a sword and buckler, for without money you can do nothing and you cannot open your mouth. You chiefs, too, of Rhodesia, listen to this word which is spoken. . . . Help us and we will fight for you. Contribute money so that we can speak to the Rhodesian Government as to the rule under which we are ruled.[20]

Proposed by an exile and with leadership to be based outside the country, this attempt was futile. But the idea of a national organization remained alive, and the first Congress in Rhodesia was founded by Aaron Jacha in 1932. Like the Voters' Association, it appealed to the elite: clerks, teachers and preachers, who accepted the rule of the settlers, but chafed under and objected to the harsh implementations of some laws—a state of affairs they tried to rectify through delegations and petitions.

By contrast, the trade union movement achieved mass appeal. Through Charles Mzingeli, the Industrial and Commercial Workers Union of South Africa (ICU) entered Rhodesia. By 1929 Mzingeli had opened a branch in Salisbury and had changed the name of the organization to the Reformed Industrial and Commercial Workers Union (RICU) to denote its independence from the mother body in the south. Despite harassment by the Administration, the RICU grew so fast in strength and popularity that it became the voice of discontent among the urban Africans, though its attempts to link the rural struggle to the urban one met with limited success. In the towns, it demonstrated to the workers the value of organization and the importance of abolishing tribal animosity between the Mandebele and the Mashona. Shamuyarira regards its "successful attempt to break down tribalism . . . as the only monumental achievement of the RICU in the history of African nationalism" in Rhodesia.[21] But by 1939, it too had become dormant. Among the reasons for its decline were inexperience, lack of an action program with a long-term objective, nonrecognition by the law,[22] and the difficulty of organizing workers who were largely migrant.

Meanwhile, all these early organizations shared a fundamental handicap. The Africans were not convinced of their importance. Since the measures taken by the settlers during the depression to protect themselves by discriminatory laws had not had their full effect or pinch, the need for these organizations was not immediately apparent to the general African populace. The war years changed the whole picture.

For both the illiterate and the educated Africans, the Second World War was an eye-opener. For one thing, it dramatized the injustice of foreign rule. How this came about can be illustrated by the story recounted by Ndabaningi Sithole, now President of the Zimbabwe African National Union (ZANU):

> "Away with Hitler! Down with him!" said the British officer.
>
> "What's wrong with Hitler?" asked the African.
>
> "He wants to rule the whole world," said the British officer.
>
> "What's wrong with that?"
>
> "He is German, you see," said the British officer, trying to appeal subtly to the African's tribal consciousness.
>
> "What's wrong with his being German?"
>
> "You see," said the British officer, trying to explain in terms that would be understandable to the African mind but failing to see its implication, "it is not good for one tribe to rule another. Each tribe must rule itself."[23]

Mainly out of loyalty to the Crown, many Rhodesian Africans enlisted and saw action in North Africa, and even in Malaya and Burma. There, they underwent experiences which shattered the myth of the white man's superiority.

> The African soldiers saw white soldiers wounded, dying, and dead. The bullet had the same effect on black and white alike. This had a very powerful psychological impact on the African. He saw what he used to call his betters suffer defeat . . . at the hands of the Germans and Japanese, and once more he was impressed by the fact that it was not being white or black that mattered but the

necessary training in these things. . . . After spending four years hunting white enemy soldiers the African never regarded them again as gods.[24]

While they took these experiences back home after the war, they did not channel them into a special-interest political movement for military veterans, even though the ex-servicemen of Rhodesia had far greater cause to be bitter than their colleagues in West Africa (who formed veterans' pressure groups). In Rhodesia, as Shamuyarira points out, they found that the very same people they had fought, the Germans and the Italians, were, as skilled immigrants, getting far better treatment than they were. The dissatisfaction of the ex-servicemen fell on deaf ears, but found a ready and sympathetic audience among their fellowmen who had not been drafted.

During the war years of unprecedented economic activity in the Rhodesias and Nyasaland, the discriminatory legislation passed in the 1930's was intensified. As land became increasingly valuable, the Land Apportionment Act had to be amended in 1941 to make it more stringent. The rise of industries caused the African population to flood the towns; therefore, the pass laws had to be rigorously implemented to control this influx. At the same time, to preserve certain jobs for the white artisans, the Industrial Conciliation Act had to be enforced. As a result of these measures, an unbridgeable gap developed between the Africans and the Europeans in terms of opportunities, wealth and status.

Such a gap, increasing in the midst of plenty, stiffened opposition among the Africans, making them conscious of common disabilities that transcended tribal ties. This was a major impetus for political and labor organizations which had been trying to unite the Africans for years. Their aims became clear and attractive not only to the elite but, more important, to the mass of the African populace. Thus in 1945, the railway workers went on strike for higher wages and better housing. Commenting on the latter, the government-appointed Tredgold Commission said: "If the present conditions in No. 2 compound are permitted to continue a day longer than can be avoided, it will be a lasting disgrace to the railway administration and to the government of this colony."[25] The disgrace lasted until the 1950's, although in the meantime the railway workers did get a wage increase.

In 1945 the African National Congress also began to revive. First led by the Reverend Thompson Samkange, then by his son, Stanlake, this political movement attracted some attention in 1948. After hesitating to lead a general strike in the main cities of Salisbury and Bulawayo, the Congress then threw itself into the struggle. It negotiated with the government; and partly through its efforts, the lot of the urban workers slightly improved. However, Congress was not in the forefront of the nationalist struggle at this time, because its leaders were still faithful to the pre-1945 methods of struggle—gentlemanly talk with the authorities without forcing their hand or embarrassing them by means of direct action like strikes and mass protests. They still believed in petitions, delegations and representations by "responsible" Africans. Such methods no longer met the needs nor fitted the mood of the Africans after 1945. Congress was out of touch.

The British African Voice Association, which was founded in 1947 by Benjamin Burombo, was more in tune with the times. It enjoyed popular support at its home base in Bulawayo and branched out from there to Salisbury. After the

1948 strike, when Burombo was the spokesman for the Bulawayo workers, he was encouraged by his success in winning a pay increase, and he started linking the urban phase of the struggle to the rural one. Here, too, discontent was rife. The implementation of the land laws drastically reduced the amount of land available to the Africans and made "squatters" out of many. Scarcity of land also forced the government to impose destocking. The Land Husbandry Act of 1951 added to the hardships by substituting individual for communal ownership. Burombo went to court to challenge the removal of the "squatters" and the implementation of the 1951 law. The law suits slowed down the government's program; in some cases, Burombo and the peasants won. To the Africans, Burombo became a hero; to the settlers a threat. The Voice Association was banned in 1952, forcing him to put aside his political activities. But he remained a symbol of African nationalism until his death in 1958, which became the occasion for a dramatic charge that the hospital had been responsible for the death of Burombo, an imposing 250-pound six-footer. The Secretary-General of the African National Congress, George Nyandoro (now Secretary-General of ZAPU) made the charge in a moving funeral speech. He was prosecuted and fined thirty-five pounds for falsely accusing the hospital administration. It was more fuel for African nationalism.

Burombo's significant legacy was the example of legal protest. Congress leaders began to challenge land laws in the courts. This had the double effect of espousing African rights and of forging ties between city and country, between elite and masses. But the Africans were still only struggling for crumbs from a white man's table that was heaped high with the benefits of the wartime boom.

CHAPTER SIX

THE RISE OF THE FEDERATION

For the Rhodesian whites, the prosperity ushered in by World War II continued into the postwar years. It was a time to bank pounds sterling in London, to transfer London affluence to Salisbury suburbs, and to build fortunes. The meaning of prosperity was dramatic and overwhelming: it established a luxury-lined vested interest for the white settler in the black man's country.

The affluence, ushered in by wartime demand for Northern Rhodesian copper, caused a sharp increase in output. This, in turn, created a heavy demand for Southern Rhodesian coal and accelerated the growth of secondary industries. Meanwhile, Nyasaland, whose main export was labor, sent more of her workers to both countries, and they remitted larger amounts of pay to their families, stimulating the economy. Among both black and white, the war was a time to make a quick kill or a fast pound sterling—though the color gap was reflected in the income gap.

The economic impact of the war was particularly noteworthy in Southern Rhodesia. Through immigration, population increased appreciably, particularly the working population. The economy became diversified as skyscrapers and factories sprouted all over. Heavy demands were made on the transportation system, but fortunately the roads built during the depression proved equal to the task, and whatever deficiencies existed in the railways were quickly set right. Skilled labor became more expensive, and being a scarce commodity, though artificially so, the skilled (i.e., European) workers occupied a strongly entrenched bargaining position.

Apart from minor setbacks the economic boom continued into the mid-1960's. Between 1949 and 1952, the national income jumped from $210 million to $356 million, and by 1964 stood at $929 million with Great Britain as the main trading partner. In 1965 imports formed 34 per cent of the national income, and exports, 38 per cent, the tobacco crop alone accounting for one third of the exports, valued at $100 million a year. In the same year, Rhodesia also exported chrome, asbestos and other minerals, for which the United States paid $11 million in 1964.[1] Sugar is also an important item in the foreign trade, bringing in some $20 million a year.

What did the boom mean for the Rhodesian whites? In its leading article, *Time* magazine described the situation in these graphic terms:

Few communities in the world can match the sun-drenched affluence that Rhodesia's hardy settlers have achieved for themselves. Lions still command the distant escarpments, and elephants, baboons and rhinos forage in the valleys of rivers bulging with hippos. But on rolling high veld, brushed with elephant grass and flowering jacaranda trees, the whites have carved out a tidy empire of modern tobacco farms and cattle ranches that has brought modest prosperity to the land. Taxes are low and so are prices; and, for whites, wages are high enough to permit all but the most menial workers their own cars, homes and servants. Salisbury, with a white population of 88,000 spread out over 30 square miles, claims more swimming pools than any U. S. city of its size.[2]

In a chapter titled "Today's Masters" the sociologist Boris Gussman tells us more about the settler's life:

> It is sometimes jokingly remarked that a pedestrian in Rhodesia is a man with only one car. It is, however, true that Southern Rhodesia has more cars proportionate to its white population than any other community in the world apart from California. Another statistic that supports the evidence for a high standard of living is that there are more millionaires in Southern Rhodesia than in Britain.

Gussman's remarks about Rhodesian drinking habits is particularly ironic, since a favorite settler complaint is that Africans drink too much: "Drinking throughout the Rhodesias is heavy by any standards. Even in South Africa where the cheapness of local wines, brandy and beers makes for a heavy expenditure on alcohol, the Rhodesians are looked upon as having an unduly pronounced partiality for the bottle."[3]

Small wonder then that any policy threatening the settlers' "paradise" would meet strong opposition and any formula for preserving it receive enthusiastic support. Such a protective device was federation of Southern Rhodesia, Northern Rhodesia and Nyasaland, an idea that was by no means new.

In 1915, the British South Africa Company proposed the amalgamation of the two Rhodesias in order to reduce the heavy costs of administration. But the Southern Rhodesian whites rejected the proposal at that time out of fear of being swamped by the huge African masses in Northern Rhodesia. Moreover, for the Southerners, the company followed in Northern Rhodesia the unacceptable policy of employing Africans in various capacities so that they were an economic threat to the European workers. Finally, the South felt that since it was near self-government, it did not want to be saddled with poor Northern Rhodesia, which had just a few Europeans and hordes of natives. But discovery of copper and other minerals in Northern Rhodesia in the 1920's made amalgamation suddenly attractive, and the objections of the South suddenly vanished. But this time the North, seeing visions of its own self-government, was cool toward the idea.

Then events in London forced the leaders in the two territories to seriously consider political amalgamation. In his memorandum[4] of 1930, Lord Passfield, better known as Sydney Webb, the Fabian Socialist, asserted the paramountcy of native interests as British policy in East Africa, and African share in government in other territories. The Hilton Young Commission of 1929 also made basically the same point.[5] Shocked and alarmed, the settler leaders in both Rhodesias started discussing "the possibility of combining the two territories in a defensive autonomy against the intrusion of such dangerous ideas."[6] Meeting at Victoria Falls in Northern Rhodesia in 1936, they decided in favor of amalgamation. As a result of this decision, the British government formed the Bledisloe Commission to inquire into the nature of the political association[7] suited for these territories.

In its 1939 report, the Commission recommended against federating the three territories because of their different constitutional structures. Northern Rhodesia and Nyasaland were British protectorates, whereas Southern Rhodesia was a self-governing territory. It also rejected the immediate amalgamation of the territories because of their differing policies toward the Africans. It said that Southern Rhodesia's policy "is in some respects restrictive and will, if persisted in, limit the opportunities open to Africans."[8] Under amalgamation this restrictive policy would be extended to the northern territories, since the South would be the dominant political partner. Indeed, in Northern Rhodesia and Nyasaland, the Commission found strong opposition to the idea and said that the "striking unanimity . . . of the native opposition to amalgamation, based mainly on dislike of some features of the native policy of Southern Rhodesia, and the anxiety of the natives in Northern Rhodesia and Nyasaland lest there should be any change in the system under which they regard themselves as enjoying the direct protection of Your Majesty, are factors which cannot in our judgment be ignored."[9]

Although World War II temporarily decreased the pressure for amalgamation, the leaders of the settlers continued their lobbying. Sir Godfrey Huggins, the Prime Minister of Southern Rhodesia, and Roy Welensky, then a leading trade unionist in Northern Rhodesia, used the Interterritorial Conference, founded by Britain to coordinate the war effort, to push for closer association of the Central African territories.[10] Most of the African opposition to this scheme came from the two northern territories. In Northern Rhodesia, Harry Nkumbula was spokesman for the opposition.

After the war, the movement for close political association

gained momentum. In 1945, Britain set up the Central African Council, a body consisting of members from the three territories to coordinate the economic activities of the territorial governments. The settlers, led by Huggins, soon saw it as a sop, a dangerous obstacle to a settler-dominated greater Rhodesia. Its danger lay in this: If it could prove economic progress to be possible without political union, then any arguments for federation would be ineffectual.

In their opposition, the settlers had luck. In May, 1948, Dr. François Malan scored a stunning electoral victory in South Africa over the revered General Smuts. His victory established Boer superiority over Briton in South Africa and threatened to embrace Rhodesia, where there was also a heavy Afrikaner element. The effect in the Rhodesias was to rule out any possibility of Anglo-Boer cooperation and any incorporation of Southern Rhodesia into the Union of South Africa. Now the three territories started thinking of federating, not amalgamating any longer. To Roy Welensky, federation had the advantage of not appearing to the Africans and their sympathizers as outright control by the settlers of the Africans.

The settlers met again at Victoria Falls in 1949 in a private conference to discuss the federation scheme. Its main attraction was that it offered a chance to rid themselves of the much-detested control of the Colonial Office, which they regarded as "soft on the Native question." As for the representation of the Africans in the proposed federation, there was to be no effective role for them; the Southern Rhodesian system of rule through the chiefs was to prevail. Rotberg quotes Malcom Barrow, a leading settler in Nyasaland, as saying that the settlers thought they could "hand over" some five million to Southern Rhodesia.[11]

The main drive for federation came from Southern Rhodesia, with its largest number of settlers and longest experience in self-government. In private talks, Huggins, the Prime Minister of Southern Rhodesia, argued for a Central African political unit in which Southern Rhodesia would naturally dominate. Such a step met strong African and humanitarian opposition. Federation was really a compromise. Central Africa was to be united in a nonindependent political structure in which the three territories would retain some control over African affairs. With the two northern territories as protectorates, this meant that Britain would have a great say. The Rhodesians only accepted this limitation because of the immense economic benefits that federation would bring them. Lord Malvern, formerly Sir Godfrey Huggins, admitted as much in 1954. Opposing a motion to grant equal treatment to all races in public places, as the preamble to the Federal Constitution required, he urged his supporters to have patience "for the sake of Federation which was for economic advancement, not for the Preamble which was forced upon us."

In London, Huggins and Welensky lobbied hard and successfully for federation. The Labour Party of Clement Attlee, then in power, agreed in principle, but was concerned to find proper safeguards for the interests of the Africans. Speaking of the difficulties of uniting Central Africa because of the differing native policies, Arthur Creech Jones, the Colonial Secretary, said: "It would be a grave misfortune if any political fusion or federation were agreed without the endorsement and goodwill of the African people and the most complete safeguards in perpetuity for them."[12] Jones, however, lost his seat in the election of 1950, and was succeeded at the Colonial Office by James Griffiths, a man with limited experience in colonial affairs. He proved no match for the wily and determined settlers. With Patrick Gordon Walker, the Secretary of State for Commonwealth Relations, Griffiths attended Victoria Falls in 1951, yet another conference with the governments of Central Africa. This one also recommended federation, despite the opposition of the Africans, who did not attend.

Late in 1951 the Conservative Party of Churchill ousted Labour from power, and reconvened in London the conference on federation. This time the Southern Rhodesian delegation included two Africans, one being Joshua Nkomo. All other Africans refused to attend. In London the conference also supported the idea and produced a draft scheme for federation. Nkomo denounced it on his return from London, but later contested a seat under the same scheme!

The case for federation was argued by Welensky in *Foreign Affairs,* October, 1952.[13] In his view, neither the African extremists, who saw their hopes for a black state dashed, nor the European extremists, who feared that the Gold Coast ideas were creeping in, would be satisfied with the scheme. But he regarded the federation as a sincere effort to devise a form of government that could make a multiracial society work with justice to all men. However, Welensky showed his hand with the qualifying statement, "Europeans in Central Africa cannot ignore the march of African nationalism, but they still have an opportunity to guide it on sane lines."[14] It is this very idea of guardianship with its implication of African inferiority that incensed African nationalists. Welensky's only contribution to the argument that political association was necessary for economic development rested on the settler feeling that the Colonial Office was far away in London and lacked awareness of local nuances and sensitivities. The argument demonstrated that a group of people, with power in their hands, will mistake their feeling that a course of action is to their advantage as justification.

Welensky's treatment of African opposition to federation is revealing. When the Africans in the northern territories, fearing subjection to the discriminatory laws of Rhodesia, asked that federation be stopped until they had parity of representation and responsibility with the Europeans, Welensky replied that the settlers could not wait that long: two to three generations would be necessary for the backward, custom-bound Africans to come up to the required standards.[15]

Without any proof, Welensky also blamed the Communists for the African fears that Britain would betray them to the settlers. In point of fact, the fears were genuine. The nationalists in the northern territories remembered how Britain had left the Africans of South Africa to the not-so-tender mercies of the Boers, despite constitutional safeguards. They knew the hardships and humiliations in South Africa and Rhodesia, and profitable though it was to work there, they had no intention of submitting permanently to discriminatory practices and indignities which would come in the wake of federation. Their fears were not allayed by the proposed African Affairs Board which would watch over legislation affecting them. The Board had no real power; it could merely make representations to the federal government and "reserve" for the pleasure of the British government legislation it considered unjust to the Africans.

The odd fact here is the rather passive acceptance of federation by the African leaders of Rhodesia. Although there was vehement and violent opposition in the northern territories, the South was calm. Nkomo served on the delegation to London, came back to denounce federation, then stood for election to the proposed Federal Parliament. As one of the African nationalists, Shamuyarira, explains it, they believed that true partnership would come, that by associating with the rather liberal Northern Rhodesia and Nyasaland, Southern Rhodesia would become more humane toward the Africans.[16] To add weight to this belief, Shamuyarira says, "Liberal groups and individual Europeans were active in the African townships, trying to convince Africans that a new era was at hand."[17] One proof of the new age was the multiracial university college to be built in Salisbury.

In short, these liberal groups, such as the Capricorn Society and the Inter-Racial Association, took the sting out of the African leadership. In bitter struggles, such groups, wittingly or unwittingly, blunt the warrior's spear by diverting attention of leaders from the immediate political struggle. Indeed, the whole approach of the Congress leadership during the formation of federation up to 1957 was to plead for equality and to request fair treatment within the existing sociopolitical order. But even then, the younger elements were restive. More out of deference to their leaders than out of conviction, they accepted federation, meanwhile organizing and biding their time.

Throughout the consideration of the federation question, the menacing figure of South Africa loomed in the background. In 1951, when Nkrumah became the first African to head a cabinet, Malan in South Africa sensed the danger to the continuance of white domination in the rest of Africa. He, therefore, strongly protested against Britain's "abdication," and went about expressing his fears to his neighbor in Rhodesia, Huggins. The latter took the cue and became increasingly fond of federation. It was viewed as a barrier against the tide of nationalism then sweeping over West Africa.

In the British Parliament, the debate reached its peak in May, 1953, when the Commons took the rare step of debating the Central Africa Bill twice in the same week. This reflected both interest and anxiety in regard to the proposed federation. In Nyasaland, there were huge demonstrations against federation, which led to deportation of Chief Gomani and the clergyman Michael Scott.

Such opposition prompted Labour to make a motion in Commons that African petitions against federation be referred to a select committee of the House and that the signatories appear in person. This was a sound motion because the Africans could never outvote the federation proposals in their own territorial parliaments where they were at the mercy of the white settlers. Under the Labour motion, the Africans could put direct pressure on the Parliament responsible for bringing the federation into legal existence. However, the Tories rejected the Labour motion, and Parliament passed the Federation Bill.

Legally, the federation was born in June, 1953; politically, it took form in Africa on September 7 of that year when Sir Godfrey Huggins resigned from the Rhodesian premiership to become the new federal premier. With two other knights, Sir Roy Welensky from Northern Rhodesia and Sir Malcom Barrow from Nyasaland, he formed the Federal Party which swallowed up most of Huggins' United Party of Rhodesia. Instead of the old hard line toward the natives, Huggins now spoke of racial partnership, a nebulous term, open to all sorts of definition. For overseas consumption, especially British, it was presented as an ideal, honestly pursued by the settlers with the support of the Africans. On the home front, partnership meant a device for throwing off the detested Colonial Office yoke in order to enable the settlers to rule Central Africa for the foreseeable future. The Africans were to be, at best, junior partners to the settlers. Huggins is even reputed to have compared the partnership to one between a horse and a rider!

To some settlers, any partnership was a step in a dangerous direction. Foreseeing African majority rule over their children, they formed the Dominion Party to strive for the implementation in Central Africa of Malan's apartheid policy. Small wonder that many of its members were Afrikaans-speaking immigrants from South Africa. At present, the Front ruling Rhodesia since 1962 consists of many former members of the Dominion Party.[18]

A yet more reactionary party appeared. This was the Confederate Party, led by a prominent lawyer, Mr. J. Dendy Young. Exclusively for white people, it was hostile to partnership, and even saw dangers in the Dominion Party's allowing a few Africans into its ranks. It favored the parallel development of black and white in separate territorial zones. This party was strongest in Southern Rhodesia.

No purely or predominantly African party appeared on the federal scene. But there was cooperation between the nationalist movements in Northern Rhodesia and Nyasaland, while their colleagues in the South were engaged in multifarious multiracial pursuits, for which they were later labeled "tea-drinkers."

An election had to be held in December 1953 to chart the course to be followed in the new federation. The three parties campaigned hard on the native question. The Federal Party put up two African candidates in Southern Rhodesia. Nkomo ran as an independent, but lost heavily. The Federal Party won by an overwhelming margin. The results were as follows:

Party	*No. Seats*	*Specially Elected Members*	
Federal	24	Europeans (for S. Rhodesia)	1
Confederates	1	Africans (for S. Rhodesia)	2
Independent	1	Africans (for N. Rhodesia and Nyasaland)	4
Dominion	0	Nominated European members (by Governors of N. R. and Nyasaland)	2

The federation's Parliament thus started out securely in the hands of the partnership school of settlers with a sprinkling of African members who were completely outnumbered and powerless. Whatever prospects of cooperation existed among the Africans were frowned upon as inimical to the spirit of partnership.[19] When in June, 1953, the newly crowned Queen gave her Royal Assent to the act forming the federation, she, in effect, pressed a crown of thorns upon the Africans and set in motion a political institution that from the very start carried within itself the seeds of its own destruction.

CHAPTER SEVEN

THE FALL OF THE FEDERATION

The federation of Rhodesia and Nyasaland stood on a shaky foundation of force. Imposed on the majority of the people of Central Africa, it lacked that most important prerequisite for stable and lasting political institutions: consent of the governed. Whatever its economic merits, the federation failed because partnership failed.

To the settlers, however, the whole scheme looked workable. They saw a means of containing African nationalism and, in Sir Roy Welensky's phrase, of guiding along "sane lines." But they underrated the strong opposition to Southern Rhodesian domination and the impact of the West African example of African rule. After Ghana became free in 1957, Nkrumah summoned his struggling brothers to come to Accra to speak of freedom. From as far afield as Basutoland and Rhodesia they trekked to Accra for the All African People's Conference of December, 1958, and it reinforced their determination. In Rhodesia, the young firebrands of the City League, James Chikerema and George Nyandoro, breathed new life into the slumbering African National Congress. In Nyasaland, Chipembere, Chiume and Dunduza Chisiza convinced the peppery physician, Hastings K. Banda, to return from Ghana to lead the struggle against the federation.

In Southern Rhodesia, the Africans had, by and large, agreed to give federation a try. With Garfield Todd as Premier, they thought that it would work, that of all politicians he was the one to feel compelled, by ties to the rather racially tolerant northern territories, to liberalize Rhodesia. Todd tried from 1953 to 1958, but his supporters thought he was going too far, and unceremoniously ousted him. Then the "tea-drinkers" woke up to the realities around them.

Another shock was the expansion of the federal Parliament. This brought about franchise qualifications so difficult that very few Africans could meet them, while embracing practically all Europeans. The African Affairs Board protested that the enlarged Parliament would diminish African representation. However, the British government ignored the protest out of deference to Welensky, who had been Prime Minister of the federation since 1956 as successor to Huggins. The latter retired after setting a record as the longest serving premier in the Commonwealth. The Queen then elevated him to the peerage and he became Lord Malvern. As some humanitarians had feared, the Board proved useless.

In Nyasaland, Banda so roused the masses against federation that violent demonstrations broke out. In February, 1959, Governor Sir Robert Armitage declared a state of emergency and jailed Banda. These developments forced the British Prime Minister Harold Macmillan to set up a commission under a judge, Sir Patrick Devlin, to inquire into the causes of the disturbances. The resulting report showed the overseas public the true facts of life behind the façade of partnership.

The Prime Minister of Rhodesia, Edgar Whitehead, took action against nationalists before Armitage. His explanation was that he was forestalling trouble. Thus, on the suspicion that they were plotting trouble against the state, five hundred ANC members were seized and held without trial, and a state of emergency was declared. Parliament then hastily passed a series of draconian laws to enable the government to deal firmly with troublemakers. These were the Unlawful Organizations Act, the Preventive Detentions Act, and the Law and Order Maintenance Act.

In the House of Commons, a Labourite often called the Member for Africa, Fenner Brockway, posed a direct question to the Conservative government concerning these laws: "Is this not an outrage? Under this legislation the most scandalous discrimination is being practiced. Does the Government refuse to protect the African population of Southern Rhodesia? . . ." The government reply was that the Rhodesian Parliament had rightly exercised the powers devolved to it over the years by successive British governments, including Labour. The scattered and fractious Labourites could give no effective rejoinder to this counter thrust, since, indeed, they had had a hand in the whole dirty business. Whitehead then calmly went about tightening his security and justifying his actions.

A Review Tribunal supported his jailing of the ANC members by finding that they had incited the Africans to violence and had planned to link their struggle with that of the nationalists in Northern Rhodesia and Nyasaland. The point on linking up is true, but it was never established and proved in open court that any ANC member had incited to violence. The ruling of the Tribunal, therefore, gave rise to the suspicions that Whitehead had fabricated the reasons for the emergency in order to pass the severe laws that would enable him to cripple the nationalist movement. An interesting sidelight was the resignation of Sir Robert Tredgold, the Chief Justice of the federation, as a sign of protest against these harsh laws, especially the Law and Order Maintenance Act. A member of an old Rhodesian family related to the Moffats of the nineteenth century, Tredgold is a highly respected member of the settler community.

Southern Rhodesia also attracted attention when African workers went on strike at the Kariba Dam project. Situated between the two Rhodesias, the dam was to cement the economic partnership between these territories and therefore was enthusiastically supported by Britain. Whitehead decided that political forces (ANC) were at work and sent troops to restore law and order. His action was suspect since it occurred about the same time as the deportation from Rhodesia of a Member of the British Parliament. John Stonehouse, a Labour MP, was visiting the federation—a common practice among British parliamentarians since they were legally responsible for this territory and had to keep informed in order to answer queries in the House as well as mail from constituents.

Whitehead complained to the federal authorities that Stonehouse had incited Africans before an ANC gathering in Salisbury. Impetuous Nyandoro had done the translating, and seems to have embellished what Stonehouse actually said. But this was (and still is) difficult to prove. Even the leader of the Opposition, Mr. Winston Field, made a poor case when he accused Stonehouse of gross irresponsibility. According to him, Stonehouse was guilty of inciting Africans to civil disobedience when he told them to behave as if the land were theirs. In July, 1959, the same matter reached the House of Lords where Lord Malvern railed against "itinerant politicians" who came to the federation to cause damage. He singled out Stonehouse—"who could speak no native tongue except Welsh"—for alarming the Africans about the horrors of federation. Although the conservative Lords upheld Malvern's case, the episode left a bad impression. If a British MP could be unceremoniously thrown out of a territory over which he was supposed to have control, what rights could the local Africans count on?

The year 1959 was truly decisive for the federation. Some settlers read the signs on the wall; others preferred to fight it out until the bitter and final end. Originally sparked by Nyasaland, the fight was really fought over Rhodesia. The turbulence sweeping through the federation in 1959 culminated in 1960 by Whitehead's calling upon all able-bodied Europeans to join the army reserve forces. He and his supporters fully realized that although economically poor Nyasaland could shout, the British government would be moved only by evidence that even the Southern Rhodesian Africans, supposedly pro-federation, were implacably opposed to federation. Without waiting for the evidence to come out publicly, Whitehead arrested the leading members of the National Democratic Party (NDP), which succeeded the banned ANC. The president Michael Mawema, the treasurer Sketchley Samkange, and Leopold Takawira, chairman of the Harare Township branch, were all arrested in 1960. So was the "moderate" vice-president of the Central Africa Party, Stanlaka Samkange, one of the "tea-drinkers" who had striven for genuine partnership. The settler government realized that African politics in Rhodesia had entered a new phase. African intellectuals, businessmen and villagers together entered the struggle under the banner of the NDP.

Whitehead had to act swiftly and firmly to preserve his hold over his Cabinet and the settler community at large. For any politician, especially one from a minority group, self-preservation is a cardinal law. From this viewpoint, there is some basis to the allegation by an NDP member, Enoch Dumbutshena, that the Rhodesian government provoked the riots of 1960 which led to the killing of twelve Africans in Bulawayo (ironically, in both Sindabele and Zulu, this word means the place of killing). The settlers had to take such stern measures since they realized that the ANC, and its successor, the NDP, had changed from polite requests for social equality to bold political demands. Dumbutshena put the NDP case in these words:

> Sir Edgar's answer to the racial tension that he himself has helped to create is to arm all whites, to carry out a crash programme of house building and to ease unemployment. That is not what Africans want. They want nothing less than a democratic government for themselves and for their children. They are not looking for the removal of pin-pricks. They want the vote, for they know that without it neither they nor their children will enjoy either peace or advancement.[1]

To settle the clash between the African nationalists and the settlers, he therefore called upon the British government to intervene, as did former Prime Minister Todd.[2]

The NDP case for British intervention gained added strength from the report of a twenty-five-man commission sent by the British government to Central Africa to study the workings of the federation and to advise on its future. Led by a peer, Viscount Monckton, after whom it was named by the press, the commission's report changed the course of the federation's history. While preoccupied with the economic hardships likely to befall the three territories if the federation were dismantled, the Monckton Report upset the Empire Loyalists and some Tories in Britain, and all the ruling settlers. It granted the territories the right to secede from the federation. "Federation cannot, in our view, be maintained in its present form. . . . No new form of association is likely to succeed unless Southern Rhodesia is willing to make drastic changes in its racial policies. . . . It appears only too likely that those who merely cling to their familiar positions will be swept away." The report also stressed that no new form of association could succeed without African support. For the settlers, these were tough words of judgment and advice; they unmistakably meant that the federation had been a failure and put the blame on Southern Rhodesia.

The curious fact is that the commission was boycotted by most Africans during its stay in Central Africa. Suspicious of settler machinations, they feared that by giving evidence they would lend an air of acceptance to whatever recommendations the commission made. Moreover, in their view the terms of reference did not seem to permit discussion on the breaking up of the federation. It is to the credit of the commissioners that they did face this ticklish but crucial question.

The only point in the report which invited criticism dealt with the Southern Rhodesian Africans. The commission found them to be in favor of federation because they hoped that the northern territories would help liberalize the South. Proof of such support was evident from the cooperation of Africans like M. Hove and J. Savanhu, the latter having become a junior minister in the federal Cabinet. In London, the federation was being represented by another African, Lawrence C. Vambe, who considered the dismantling of the federation to be detrimental to African interests. He said, "There is some evil genius behind the break-up-the-Federation campaign who wants to bring about suffering and despair among the African people."[3] In the absence of evidence to the contrary, the commission concluded that there was widespread African support for federation in Southern Rhodesia.

The NDP immediately pounced on this point. In London, T. G. Silundika issued a statement which said:

> We resent most strongly the fabricated conclusion by the Commission that Africans in Southern Rhodesia favour Federation and did not boycott the Commission. It should be recalled that in 1952 Mr. Nkomo was sent to London by the African people to oppose the formation of the Federation. One of the main reasons given by the Whitehead regime for banning the A.N.C., then led by Mr. Nkomo, was that it opposed Federation. From its inception the present National Democratic Party has declared for a policy of breaking up Federation. In line with this, the N.D.P. announced and carried out its total boycott of the Commission. The Africans who are referred to as favouring Federation are the few who receive regular payment from the Government in order to support white supremacy.

Despite this shortcoming, due in part to the Africans themselves, the Monckton Report shattered settler hopes of continuing their rule. As Minister of Central African Affairs, the unflappable R. Butler calmly supervised the dismantling of the federation after a decade of a stormy life. First Nyasaland, then Northern Rhodesia, opted out.

But in Rhodesia, the settlers had long seen the writing on the wall. In his "winds of change" speech in Cape Town, Macmillan had convinced diehard Rhodesian segregationists that, if pressed enough, Britain would not hesitate to bow to demands for independence. But Britain found herself attacked from both quarters: to the Africans, she was moving too slow; to the settlers, she was rushing headlong to rack and ruin. In Whitehead's proposed amendment to the Land Apportionment Act and in the easing of other discriminatory measures, the settler diehards saw the opening wedge of dreaded African rule—in their lifetime, too. Moreover, ineffable horrors erupted in the neighboring Belgian Congo, until then widely regarded by other colonial powers as an oasis of calm in a continent otherwise ravaged by the storms of nationalism.

To some frightened and, indeed, unsettled settlers, Whitehead and his United Federal Party were soft on the native question. True enough, he had acted firmly and swiftly to stave off another Congo by arresting the troublemakers in Salisbury. But the specter of another Congo in Rhodesia itself was raised in the Rhodesian press, a good portion of which was owned and directed by South African tycoons. These unsettling events led to a drop in Whitehead's popularity and a rise in influence of Winston Field's Dominion Party. But before Field and Whitehead confronted each other in an election, the NDP's lobbying in London resulted in a conference for drawing up a new constitution for Rhodesia.

Held in Salisbury in February 1961, the conference was

unprecedented. For the first time in Rhodesia's history, a Prime Minister and African leaders sat down together to discuss the future of their country—though African participation was achieved only after protracted negotiations. Under Whitehead's chairmanship, the conference was attended by the United Federal Party, the Dominion Party, the Central Africa Party and the National Democratic Party, represented by Joshua Nkomo and the Reverend Nabaningi Sithole. Advocate Herbert Chitepo, Enos Nkala and Silundika acted as their advisers. The Coloured and Asiatic Peoples also participated. On rather minor points the conference reached agreement, but deadlocked on the franchise. The NDP wanted universal suffrage; the CAP, a qualified vote; the DP, no change at all in the existing arrangement. The UFP presented a compromise proposal. As if by prearrangement, at this stage, the Secretary of State for Commonwealth Relations, Duncan Sandys, came to Salisbury to assume chairmanship of the Conference. The UFP's proposal was eventually accepted.

In a referendum, the Rhodesian voters approved the new constitution by a large majority, and in December, 1961, the House of Commons accepted it, too. It replaced the 1923 Constitution, but did not change the status of Rhodesia as a self-governing colony. Hence the executive authority remained vested in the Governor, the Queen's representative; whereupon Sir Humphrey Gibbs, a Rhodesian of old descent, became Governor.

The salient features of this Constitution can be summarized under three headings: (1) Britain's reserved powers, (2) franchise and (3) representation. Under this Constitution, Britain's reserved powers under the 1923 Constitution were to be relinquished; these mainly affected laws held to be discriminatory against Africans and, anyhow, were never used in the whole of Rhodesia's history. Some powers, however, were still reserved. For example, Rhodesia could not abolish the formal powers of the Governor; nor could she have a free hand in her international relations if these clashed with Britain's interests. In theory, too, Britain could still legislate for the colony, though in practice she was to act only with the consent of the Rhodesian government.

To replace the reserved powers, a Declaration of Rights was written into the 1961 Constitution. A Constitutional Council was also set up to examine bills passed by the Parliament before they reached the Governor for his signature. But Parliament could overrule the Council by a two-thirds majority or by a simple majority vote after a delay of six months. Moreover, Parliament could pass a law without submitting it to the Council if it received a "certificate of urgency" from the government. Subsequently, the Council could examine the enacted law, and in case it disagreed, Parliament had to decide to repeal or amend that law. In short, the Council had very little effective power.

The Declaration of Rights formed a long section of the Constitution. Its stated aim was to provide for fundamental rights for all people irrespective of race or color or creed. But protection of these rights was qualified and restricted. It was subject to the public interest; it did not apply to laws in force before November 1, 1962; nor did it apply to money matters. This meant that all the obnoxious laws in the statute book were to remain, and that in case of a state of emergency the government had full latitude. In short, all the laws and practices already existing were to be left unaffected by the Declaration.

The Constitution's provision for voting was a distinctive example of the "fancy franchise," one of Britain's unique creations for her racially heterogeneous colonies. Viewed superficially, the franchise is nonracial, and indeed, the supporters of the Front made the most propaganda capital out of this point. But close inspection of the voting provisions reveals a totally different picture. The electorate was divided into two categories: the A roll and the B roll. To qualify for the A roll, which elected 50 of the 65 members of the Assembly, the voter had to possess (a) an income of £792 for each of the two preceding years or immovable property worth £ 1,650; (b) an income of £528 again for the two previous years or property valued at £1,100 and a complete primary education; (c) an income of £330 or property worth £550 and a secondary education. Finally, appointment as chief or headman automatically placed one on this roll.

For the B roll, the qualifications were less stringent: (a) income of £264 during the previous half-year or ownership of immovable property valued at £495; (b) income of £132 during the previous six months or property valued at £275 and two years of secondary education. For those over the age of thirty, the qualifications for this roll included an income of £132 or ownership of property valued at £275 and a primary education; otherwise an income of £198 or ownership of property worth £385. Finally, ministers of religion and kraal heads with a following of twenty or more heads of families automatically qualified. The educational facilities in Rhodesia being weighted in favor of the Europeans and the economic power being firmly in their hands, it was inevitable that the settlers would dominate the A roll. On the basis of these voting qualifications, the number of registered voters reported in Parliament in August, 1964, were as follows:

Racial Group	*A Roll*	*B Roll*
Europeans	89,278	608
Africans	2,263	10,466
Coloreds	1,308	176
Asians	1,231	114
	94,080	11,364

The flagrant imbalance in voting strength between Europeans and Africans led some defenders of the regime to hold that if African nationalists were to stop boycotting the Constitution, 7,000 people (Africans) would be added to the A roll. But lifting the boycott would solve little, for there would still be an outrageous discrepancy: 89,000 Europeans as against 9,000 Africans in a country where the latter outnumbered the former by 4,000,000 to 220,000.

Clearly, the Constitution did not envisage quick African majority rule. It was designed, according to the British view, to phase the process over many years before independence could be granted to Rhodesia. In the settlers' view, on the other hand, this was an independence constitution. Later, it became clear to the African participants that the settlers had agreed to their representation in Parliament merely to gain independence from Britain, and then to continue their old policies without the hated control, however tenuous, of the British government.

Another crucial section of the Constitution deals with amendments. This was possible only by a two-thirds majority vote of the Assembly. But if there were to be an amendment of one of the entrenched clauses dealing with the judges, the

Declaration, the Constitutional Council, then in addition each of the four racial groups in the country had to approve the amendment in a separate referendum. The important consideration here was whether, in such a case, the rural areas controlled by government-paid chiefs would count more in the opinion of the government than the towns. During the conference, there were fears, later proved correct, that the settlers would regard the voice of the chiefs as truly representative of African opinion. Nonetheless, the atmosphere immediately after the Constitutional Conference in February, 1961, was extremely friendly. Except for the Rhodesian Front, all the participants including the NDP accepted the Constitution. Jubilant and satisfied with the safeguards, Nkomo even broadcast to the country on government radio services. The NDP attitude was that a Constitutional Conference under British auspices would stress Britain's responsibility to the Africans and tend to weaken the power of the settlers.

However, the atmosphere of harmony did not last long. In the United Federal Party, Mr. Ian Smith, the Chief Whip, resigned in protest against the liberal provisions of the Constitution. The Dominion Party openly dissociated itself from the decisions reached at the conference (but later accepted the Constitution when it became law). In the NDP, Takawira and Mawema condemned Nkomo and Sithole for accepting it and were immediately suspended from the party. Then on February 17, 1961, Nkomo and Sithole announced their total rejection of the constitutional proposals on the grounds that the terms offered for African participation in government did not, as they had been led to believe, form an acceptable basis for working toward majority rule. Explaining the new turn in the NDP, Nkomo said, "A leader is he who expresses the wishes of his followers; no sane leader can disregard the voice of his people and supporters." He then rescinded the suspension of Takawira and Mawema.

Nkomo was attacked by the UFP for weakening Whitehead's hand in his efforts to ban racial discrimination in public places and to repeal the Land Apportionment Act. In some African circles, his leadership became suspect. Viewing the new situation, *The Times* (London) of February 18,1961, noted:

> The implications are grave. The Southern Rhodesia agreement which the right-wing European Dominion Party refused to accept from the start, now lacks also the support of the only African nationalist party represented at the conference table. It is in short a dead letter, and it will not be surprising if Sir Edgar Whitehead, Prime Minister of Southern Rhodesia, sees in this a strong argument for Southern Rhodesia's secession from the Federation.

The NDP then instituted a boycott of the Constitutional referendum. But in July, 1961, the registered voters approved the Constitution anew by 41,949 votes to 21,846. The settlers were satisfied that it left effective power in their hands and would lead to African majority rule only if they wanted it—and this was most inconceivable. Nkomo and the NDP rejected the new Constitution because they felt that it was a fraud. They argued that in racially divided Rhodesia, any proposed improvement in race relations had to have a special appeal to the oppressed African masses. In their view, the Constitution failed dismally in this important respect. The collision course was, therefore, set.

CHAPTER EIGHT

THE GATHERING STORM OVER UDI

The rejection of the 1961 Constitution by the NDP was a sign of trouble for the government and a source of strength for the party. African nationalists in Rhodesia were further helped by the rising discontent in town and country. In the reserves, the Land Apportionment and Husbandry Acts were causing hardships; land was becoming increasingly scarce for the burgeoning African population. And in the towns, jobs were becoming scarce as the uncertain political situation discouraged investment. Nkomo, Sithole and other NDP leaders had a ready audience.

In their tour of the country to urge a boycott of the referendum and the elections, the NDP leaders drew increasing support. African intellectuals, workers and rural villagers rallied around the party, swelling its membership. They saw the party program as the path toward victory over the settlers and toward a better life. By the end of 1961 NDP membership was estimated at 200,000.

The rising nationalist tide also caused waves of violence. When the government-paid chiefs organized rival meetings in the countryside, scuffles broke out; hecklers were manhandled. In the towns, for an African to be neutral or on the side of the government was a hazardous undertaking. It was considered treason to the cause; hence, the African members of the federal Parliament were deeply resented, even despised by their fellow Africans.

Government reaction, in turn, was swift and hard. Weekend meetings in the rural areas were banned unless the organizers obtained a special permit. In August, 1961, all African political meetings were banned. Still, the Africans did meet. At one such illegal meeting in Bulawayo in October, the police used tear gas and even opened fire, killing one person.

The African reaction against the 1961 Constitution caused some liberal-minded white Rhodesians, led by Mr. Todd and Dr. Ahrn Palley, to form the New Africa Party in August, 1961. Their aim was to amend the Constitution so as to lead to the formation of a genuine government of, by and for Europeans and Africans—a constructive idea, but it came too late to catch on. Mutual fear and mistrust were too deeply embedded by now on both sides of the color line. There was hardly any place for "moderates." The prevailing spirit can be gauged from these developments: moderate Africans like Stanlake Samkange and Nathan Shamuyarira refused to serve on the Constitutional Council; so did the former federal Chief Justice, Sir Robert Tredgold. The position of African members of the federal Parliament, Hove and Savanhu, became more untenable by the day.

Meanwhile, as the NDP leaders were in Dar es Salaam for Tanganyika's independence celebrations, Nkomo heard that Whitehead had banned the NDP. Undaunted, Nkomo announced on December 18 the formation of the Zimbabwe African People's Union, ZAPU, with himself as President. His deputy was the physician Dr.Tichafa S. Parirenyatwa, a new figure in Rhodesian politics, but an old hand in the politics of the African National Congress of South Africa. He had been an active member of the Congress' Youth League during his medical studies at the University of Witwatersrand in Johannesburg. Also on the ZAPU Executive were Sithole, Nyandoro, Mawema and Chikerema. While continuing along the principles laid down for the NDP, ZAPU added a new touch by stressing the need to project the Rhodesian struggle onto the international scene. There was to be greater focus on the Pan-African aspects of the struggle and on the role of the United Nations, a strategy warranted by the increasing importance of the new states of Africa and Asia.

ZAPU[1] clashed with Whitehead from the very beginning, because it represented a direct challenge to settler dominance. Whitehead used all the rigors of the law to crush it. He extended the 1961 ban on political meetings to 1962 and banned several of its members from addressing gatherings. Some defied these bans and were arrested. Then in January, 1962, the police opened fire to disperse a gathering in Salisbury, and later the government published a White Paper accusing the ZAPU Youth League[2] of organizing a wave of violence, arson and sabotage. Although not altogether justified, the charges did have some basis. As Shamuyarira relates,[3] ZAPU did have a core of young saboteurs.

After announcing that he had decided "to make a quick end to the present wave of acts of violence and sabotage," Whitehead banned ZAPU on September 20, 1962. At the same time, some 1,600 Africans were arrested, and 300 served with orders restricting their movements. Away in Lusaka, Nkomo announced that far from disbanding ZAPU he was setting up a government-in-exile in Dar es Salaam. This decision caused consternation among the militant members in his Executive who felt that the struggle had to be continued underground in Rhodesia. After some hesitation, he decided to return home and was immediately arrested and confined to his birthplace in the reserves. Not for the first time, there were deep doubts about Nkomo's leadership that would later cause some of his followers to break away.

In the meantime, the Whitehead regime tried to appeal to moderate white and African opinion in the coming election under the 1961 Constitution. To his party, the UFP, he announced that stern measures would be taken to deal with African extremists and received the party's support for the gradual abolition of the Land Apportionment Act, a major cause of racial strife in Rhodesia. He also promised to outlaw racial discrimination in public places. Through such concessions, he argued, it would be possible for Britain to grant independence to the country and to preserve white leadership.

To the Rhodesian Front, formed by Mr. Ian Smith in March, 1962, out of members of the old Dominion Party and influential farmers and businessmen who disagreed with the UFP, these proposed changes were unacceptable. Charging the UFP with opening the way to an African take-over, the Front decided to campaign against going too far and too fast to appease world opinion and the Africans. The mood of the campaign was reflected by the following slogan shouted by a heckler at Sir Roy, when he spoke in favor of the UFP at a Salisbury rally: "Vote Rhodesian Front for a White Christmas."[4] The slogan proved highly effective, and brought the settlers a white Christmas—and more. In the December, 1962, election, the Front, led by Mr. Winston Field, a prominent farmer, obtained 54 per cent of the mostly white votes. The results stood thus:

A Roll:	Rhodesian Front	35 seats	(all Europeans)
	UFP	15 seats	(14 Europeans, 1 African)
B Roll:	UFP	14 seats	(13 Africans, 1 Colored)
	Independent	1 seat	(European)

The results sounded the death knell for the moderates. The Central African Party, which had earlier dismissed Todd for advocating British intervention in Rhodesia, was completely wiped out and decided to disband. Led by ZAPU nationalists, most Africans boycotted the election. The lone Independent elected on the B roll was a European, Dr. Palley, who stood in a predominantly African constituency in Salisbury. His election was a tribute to his efforts as a fighter for African rights. The few Africans on the electoral register, therefore, decided to put their trust in him. As later events proved, the confidence was not misplaced.

This was a crucial election for the tottering federation and for shaky Rhodesia itself. It struck the last blow at the federation, for now neither Northern Rhodesia nor Nyasaland could possibly work with a government openly dedicated to thwarting African advancement. For Britain, the victory enormously increased her difficulties in dealing with Rhodesia.[5] She could no longer argue at the United Nations that European leadership in Rhodesia was moving speedily toward majority rule because the Front stood for "polite apartheid." Had the UFP won, Rhodesia would probably have obtained independence like the northern territories.

Since independence was the goal of successive Rhodesian governments, and the UFP approach enjoyed Britain's blessing and would have entrenched settler interests perhaps forever, why did Whitehead lose the election? Basically, the proposed relaxation of the repressive measures thorougly alarmed the white electorate. They pictured Africans building homes anywhere they wanted and even attending the same schools as whites. This dreaded socializing was, they felt, bound to lead to miscegenation and other settler nightmares. As to the possibility that the UFP approach was merely a tool for hoodwinking the British government into granting independence on terms which the settlers would later be free to ignore, the Front suspected that the British would outmaneuver them. The Africans were equally suspicious of Britain, but for the opposite reason: they felt that she was setting up another South Africa in collusion with the settlers. The memory of the protracted and notorious Treason Trial in South Africa (1956–1961) was still too fresh, and a reminder of Britain's role in the suffering of their brothers. In 1910 Britain had granted South Africa independence with entrenched constitutional guarantees for African interests but let South Africa ride roughshod over these guarantees. Now, amidst the subsequent exploitation of the Africans, Britain was unashamedly extracting huge profits while simultaneously denouncing apartheid! Could the same not happen in Rhodesia?

UFP also failed to understand the African mood. To ZAPU and other nationalists, Sir Edgar's campaign pledges merely dealt with social reforms, whereas the African leadership wanted real political power. In the 1950's African leaders would have jumped at such promises; now, they rejected them outright. Nkomo summed up the new mood when, after the courts had ruled that segregation in public swimming pools was illegal, he said, "We don't want to swim in your swimming pools. We want to swim with you in Parliament." Hence the effectiveness of the boycott. Out of the roughly 3,600,000 Rhodesian Africans in 1962, 60,000 were eligible to vote. Of these, 50,000 refused to register, and 7,000 who were already on the register boycotted the election. The boycott thus deprived the electoral results of whatever semblance of African participation they might otherwise have had; the fourteen African Members of Parliament were elected in white constituencies.

The composition of the new Cabinet reflected the Front's get-tough approach. Field became Prime Minister, while king-maker Ian Smith took charge of the Treasury. London-born Clifford Dupont took over the controversial Ministry of Justice, while Calcutta-born William Harper was widely regarded as the architect of the Front's racial policies. These were the leading hard-liners in the Front who wanted independence at any price for Rhodesia and who became known as the "Cowboys."

The Front's policies were clear from the start of its rule in 1963. On the one hand, it freed Nkomo and other 1959 detainees and did not renew the restriction on those subsequently arrested. On the other hand, it proposed amendments to the Law and Order (Maintenance) Act, the Unlawful Organizations Act and the Native Affairs Act. One of these amendments introduced the death sentence for the use of explosives, and was aimed at ZAPU saboteurs. It was strenuously but unsuccessfully opposed by the Opposition. Since Mr. Field said that these new measures were urgent, the Constitutional Council could not pass on them. A sign of the times was the expulsion of Dr. Terence Ranger, a history lecturer at the University College who had fought in the nationalist ranks. Virtually, the whole country was kept on its toes—alert, fearful and ready for war, especially from within.

With the federation clearly moribund, Sir Roy and Field asked Britain for the same right to independence as Northern Rhodesia and Nyasaland. Toward this end, they held talks in London in April, 1963, followed in July by a conference at Victoria Falls. For "Rab" Butler, Minister for Central African Affairs, and his Conservative colleagues in the government, this request posed a dilemma. The younger Conservatives like the Bow Group and Humphrey Berkeley opposed Rhodesia's independence unless there was greater provision for African representation; the others pressed for recognition of Rhodesia's right to freedom because they feared that, if rebuffed, the settlers would carry out their long-standing threat of union with South Africa. To lend credibility to this fear, Sir Roy in May, 1963, went to South Africa ostensibly on a "fishing trip" with Prime Minister Verwoerd. What he caught nobody knows, but the meeting of the two fishermen sent temperatures rising in Whitehall. There were suspicions that the settlers were seeking advice and aid for the impending unilateral declaration of independence if Britain refused to grant the regime's demands. What was Britain to do? Hand over power to the settlers in the hope that the warring factions would in freedom find unity? Such a hope had inspired Britain's magnanimity toward South

Africa after the Anglo-Boer War (1899–1902) and had resulted in the Africans' subjection.[6] The alternative of denying this right to Rhodesia seemed equally fraught with difficulties. Butler's solution was to stall for time by ruling that further talks were necessary. Thus, there began that series of meetings which proved inconclusive and led to Field's ouster, and ultimately to UDI.

Meanwhile, there was growing African discontent, following the banning of ZAPU. Matters were made worse by unemployment and continued arrests. It was revealed in Parliament that whereas in 1963 there had been 1,168 arrests under the Law and Order Maintenance Act, there were 1,449 during the first six months of 1964. Convinced that these arrests would cripple the work of ZAPU at a time when UDI was pending, Nkomo urged his Executive to escape to Dar es Salaam so as to be ready to form a government-in-exile there when UDI came. Jumping bail and other restriction conditions, many of them made the arduous trip only to discover that such a move had no support among the other African leaders, especially President Nyerere, who urged them to go back and struggle at home.

Once again, Nkomo's leadership was doubted. This time, however, consequences were grave, for some of Nkomo's colleagues felt that they had reached the parting of the ways. They disagreed with Nkomo's policy of fighting from outside or "circumvention" and instead urged him to face the government squarely—"confrontation." This line of action was urged on him on his return to Salisbury in July, 1963, by Enos Nkala, Shamuyarira and nine other ZAPU members. Nkomo stood his ground and the ZAPU ranks split asunder.[7]

Supporting the dissenters in Salisbury were four former

ZAPU members in Dar es Salaam: The Reverend N. Sithole, Robert Mugabe, Leopold Tawawira and Washington Malianga. After Nkomo had publicly denounced them all as traitors, they set about undermining his leadership. Sithole and Takawira returned from Dar es Salaam to organize the efforts to unseat Nkomo. But with his political life at stake, Nkomo outmaneuvered them, thwarted their efforts and retained substantial support, especially in the rural areas. The factional fight within the ranks of the African nationalists resulted in violence and led to the formation of the Zimbabwe African National Union (ZANU) in August, 1963. Sithole became president and led an executive consisting of all the former dissenters who now included Advocate Herbert Chitepo. This split into ZANU and ZAPU was to divide not only the Africans in Rhodesia, but also their supporters in the newly formed Organization of African Unity—some favoring Nkomo; others, Sithole.

In Rhodesia, the only people to profit from the intraparty squabble were white settlers and their regime. It enabled Mr. Field and his colleagues to concentrate on their efforts to obtain independence from Britain relatively free of the accusation that they were riding roughshod over the African populace. For were not the Africans themselves at each other's throats? But Mr. Field's efforts bore no fruit. To the "Cowboys," he seemed a victim of the wiles of the British and was trying to beat them at their own game—talking. In April, 1964, he resigned as Prime Minister because, in his words, "A serious difference of opinion has arisen between the party members in Parliament and myself over the policy to be followed, and I have been requested to make room for somebody else."[8] The "somebody else" was Ian Smith, the Finance

Minister. Born in Rhodesia in 1919 and educated at Rhodes University in South Africa, Smith came into prominence in 1961 when he resigned as Chief Whip of the UFP over the Constitution. He then helped found the Rhodesian Front Party to oppose further political concessions to Africans. Now as successor to Field, he was leading the "Cowboys."

One of Smith's first acts was to break the back of the nationalist movement through mass arrests and restrictions. ZANU and the PCC-ZAPU[9] were banned; so was the pro-nationalist publication, *The Daily News*. After serving terms of imprisonment, both Nkomo and Sithole were sent to restriction camps—Nkomo to Gonakudzingwa, near the Mozambique border, and Sithole to Sikombela, some 190 miles from Salisbury. By the end of 1964 an estimated 1,980 Africans were in detention or restriction. But far from dispirited, the detainees made the best use of their forced togetherness. There was a daily schedule of physical training, political discussions and academic training. For example, Sithole used his time to take a correspondence course for a degree in sociology.

Regarding Britain, the Smith Government continued negotiations for independence, but took an increasingly inflexible attitude. It rejected proposals to increase African representation in Parliament, which would speed up the process to majority rule. Instead, it threatened to declare Rhodesia's independence by Christmas if negotiations proved fruitless. Such a threat rested on the conviction that the majority of the white Rhodesians supported UDI. However, the former federal Prime Minister, Sir Roy Welensky, disagreed with this approach, and in August, 1964, came out of retirement to form the Rhodesia Party (RP), whose policy was to gain independence by negotiation. In a by-election for the safe RP seat of Arundel near Salisbury, Sir Roy presented himself as candidate in order to disprove the government's contention that the majority wanted independence by illegal means if necessary. To prove its point, the Front chose no less a man than the Deputy Prime Minister, Clifford Dupont, to stand against Sir Roy. Dupont won by 1,079 votes against Welensky's 446.

One reason for the Front's victory was the London meeting held just before the election between Smith and Sir Alec Douglas-Home. They issued a joint communique which showed that there was no immediate danger of UDI, thereby taking the steam out of Sir Roy's campaign. But the more important reason was the emergence of the independent states of Zambia (formerly Northern Rhodesia) and Malawi (formerly Nyasaland). To the settlers this meant that the dreaded African rule was at their doorsteps. To meet this danger, Welensky, in the settlers' opinion, came up with a wishy-washy program, whereas the Front represented toughness, kragdadigheid, the very quality badly needed for coping with the rise of a similar danger within the borders of Rhodesia. After his defeat, Sir Roy retired in order to tend his roses and write his memoirs.

The Front's victory over the RP at Arundel and in another by-election was hailed in South Africa, where Smith had visited Dr. Verwoerd and his Foreign Minister, Dr. Muller, in July. Their private talks ended in a new trade agreement between the two countries, but it was widely believed that they had also exchanged views on UDI. In September, another member of the Unholy Triumvirate, Don Salazar, received in Lisbon a courtesy visit from Smith, who was on his way to London for yet another round of talks on independence. The choice of Lisbon before London was seen in Opposition circles as a deliberate snub of Britain and as a mark of solidarity of the southern African rulers.

The government's crackdown on remnants of African opposition continued without break. Not even Mr. Justice Dendy Young's ruling that Nkomo and his colleagues were illegally restricted stopped the government. When it lost on appeal, the new Minister of Justice, South-African born and bred Desmond Lardner-Burke, told Parliament on August 13, 1964, that Nkomo and his colleagues would be detained in the public interest.

Then the government summoned a so-called *indaba,* or consultation of chiefs. From October 22 to 26, some six hundred chiefs, invited by the government to represent African opinion, gathered at Domboshawa near Salisbury to be polled on the Front's policy. To forestall trouble during the consultation, the public and the press were excluded and troops called up to clear the surrounding area of "undesirable elements." The chiefs dutifully rejected the "one man, one vote" call, and asked for Rhodesia's independence under the Constitution. However, the Conservative government in Britain soon made it clear that it did not consider this method of consultation representative of African opinion.

For the registered voters, the government used a referendum. They were asked on November 4 whether or not they favored independence under the 1961 Constitution. The Front won easily. The predominantly white electorate of 105,628 voters consisted of A Roll, 89,886, and B Roll, 12,729. In the referendum 58,091 voted *Yes*, 6,906 *No*, and 944 votes were declared invalid. This result, the Front quickly pointed out, would have been enough in an election to give them all the 50 seats on the A Roll plus the two-thirds majority required for an amendment to the Constitution. To strengthen his hand in negotiation by gaining such a majority, Smith decided to hold a general election on May 7, 1965. Concentrating only on the A Roll seats, the Front swept the polls and gained all these seats. On the B Roll, the Rhodesia Party returned 10 Africans; there were also 5 Independents: 3 Africans, 1 Indian and 1 European—Dr. Ahrn Palley. The 10 Africans of the RP decided to form a new multiracial party, the United People's Party, under Mr. Josiah Gondo, who became the leader of the Opposition in Parliament.

Ironically, the swing to the Front produced exactly the opposite result from that originally envisaged by Whitehead and Duncan Sandys in framing the supposedly nonracial 1961 Constitution. Now there was a racial confrontation. Clearly, the Constitution was unworkable. To grant independence under it was dangerous and justified the concern of critics at home and abroad (especially at the United Nations).

Far from demonstrating support for the Front on independence under this Constitution, the election, in fact, strengthened the nationalist demand for a conference to draw up a new constitution granting more representation to the Africans on the important A Roll. Since their plea had been repeatedly rejected, the nationalists continued their boycott; only 2,530 votes had been cast on the B Roll. Numerically, the newly formed United People's Party was too small to deprive the government of a two-third vote on any measure, including a constitutional amendment. The party was also weak in sheer ability and experience. Mr Gondo had little knowledge of the workings of government, though his deputy, Mr. Chad Chipunza, was better equipped, having served as a Parliamentary Secretary in the federal government in the days of Welensky. A source of strength was Dr. Palley, a physician and a lawyer by training. His wife, Dr. Claire Palley, was one of Rhodesia's leading constitutional experts and taught law at the University College in Salisbury.

From July onward, the number of talks between Rhodesia and Britain on independence increased in search of a compromise. Smith suggested widening the B Roll so as to embrace all African taxpayers and creating an Upper House of twelve chiefs who would vote with the Assembly on bills amending the entrenched clauses of the Constitution. He even added a solemn treaty of adherence to the principles and spirit of the 1961 Constitution—but refused to repeal the Land Apportionment Act. All the proposals of the Rhodesians, while no doubt made in good faith, just skirted the main issue. Extending the B Roll did not mean an increase in the number of people elected—more Africans would elect the fifteen members on this roll. The inclusion of chiefs was immediately suspect, since the chiefs depended on the government for their positions and pay. The British proposals, made by the new Labour government of Harold Wilson and Arthur Bottomley at the Commonwealth Relations Office, were unacceptable to Smith.

In desperation, Wilson and Bottomley flew to Rhodesia in October, 1965. They met with Smith, and then met Nkomo and Sithole, whom they urged in vain to use the 1961 Constitution. Finally, Wilson proposed the setting up of a Royal Commission under the Rhodesian Chief Justice, Sir Hugh Beadle, to propose amendments to the 1961 Constitution. But Wilson and Smith had diametrically opposed views of the Commission's task. For the latter, the Commission was to find out whether the Rhodesian people wanted, in gaining independence, the 1961 Constitution with the proposed amendments. As pointed out earlier, these were unacceptable to Britain. More talking was necessary.

However, the Front had long made plans for action in case these talks failed. In November, import and export regulations were tightened, a sign that UDI was just round the corner. On November 5, a state of emergency was declared for the whole country. Then on November 11, with police and the armed forces on the alert, Smith and his colleagues announced that they were unilaterally declaring the independence of Rhodesia from Britain. The illegal deed was done.

CHAPTER NINE

RHODESIA AND THE UNITED NATIONS

It was in the United Nations that the Rhodesian question was laid bare with all its complications and its challenge to the gap between principle and practice in international diplomacy. For Great Britain, it was a test of the rationale which she offered as justification for her Rhodesian policy. For Asia and Africa, it was a reminder of the realities of geopolitics. For West and East, it sometimes became an opportunity to join their struggle on another battleground. Certainly few other issues before the United Nations have demonstrated with such clarity the practice of self-interest in national policy and the refusal to act even on issues that violate the very principles on which the international organization was founded.

All this was evident from the UN's first confrontation with the Rhodesian problem in 1961 during the Sixteenth Session of the General Assembly. As the result of a petition by Nkomo, the Afro-Asian states in the Fourth (Trusteeship) Committee submitted to the General Assembly a draft resolution asking the Special Committee of Seventeen (later expanded to Twenty-Four) to consider whether Southern Rhodesia had attained a full measure of self-government. The matter was postponed until February, 1962, when the United Kingdom delegation made known its stand under two headings: principle and fact. The principle, she argued, was that Rhodesia lay beyond the competence of the United Nations and only the United Kingdom had responsibility over this territory. In other words, Rhodesia was a colony of Britain. But the fact of the matter, the delegation pointed out, was that since 1923 Rhodesia had enjoyed a special autonomous status with wide international recognition; this status consisted in full control over its internal affairs. Therefore, Rhodesia was not obliged to provide Britain with information on her economic, social and educational policies; nor did Britain have the legal power to demand such information. The plain fact was that the United Kingdom could not give what it did not have, asserted her Permanent Representative.

To the Afro-Asian states, newly emerged from colonial rule, the British government's argument was unconvincing and threadbare. As an African diplomat put it to the author in 1965, the British were trying to hide behind a bush with no leaves. On one hand, Rhodesia was a colony; therefore, Britain alone was responsible. On the other hand, Rhodesia was self-governing; therefore, Britain had no authority. How could there be a semi-independent colony? Both question and answer proved baffling and elusive.

Ghana, Guinea, the Ivory Coast, Liberia, Nigeria, Tanganyika and Sierra Leone were joined by the Soviet Union in attacking the British stand. They argued that self-government by a minority violated the principles of the United Nations; hence Rhodesia fell within the jurisdiction of the organization. On the facts of the matter, they stressed in debate that Britain had submitted to the United Nations information on other territories even though, at the time, they too had self-government. Why, then, was Rhodesia different? Was it because Rhodesia was ruled by white people closely related to Britain? From the start, this suspicion underlay the UN debates.

To the "kith and kin" charge, Britain replied that the 1961 Constitution contained sound provisions for safeguarding African interests. She referred to the Declaration of Rights, the Constitutional Council and the pledges by the Rhodesian Prime Minister, Sir Edgar Whitehead. But in the very Constitution, the Afro-Asian states saw the entrenchment of minority rule. The voters on the A Roll had fifty seats, the number required for the two-thirds majority needed to amend the constitution. The Fourth Committee accepted the draft resolution on determining the extent of Rhodesian self-government and then recommended the resolution to the General Assembly for adoption. In February the Assembly did so, in Resolution 1745.

From March to May the Special Committee concerned itself with Rhodesia, hearing statements by the petitioners Nkomo (ZAPU), Paul Mushonga (Zimbabwe National Party), and Mr. Garfield Todd, former Prime Minister of

Rhodesia. It also set up a Subcommittee on Rhodesia to remain in touch with the British government and to discuss future action. Consisting of India, Mali, Tanganyika, Tunisia and Venezuela, with Mr. C. S. Jha of India as chairman, the Subcommittee visited London in April at the invitation of the British Government. In its report, it said that Rhodesia was not fully self-governing; that the 1961 Constitution needed revision, since it did not provide adequately for African representation; and proposed that Britain be asked to convene another conference to draw up a new constitution. In June, 1962, the findings of the Subcommittee, which described the situation in Rhodesia as grave and urgent, were incorporated in a resolution of the General Assembly.

In October, the Fourth Committee again took up Rhodesia. Petitioners from Rhodesia came to make statements: Reverend Michael Scott, Dumbutshena, Sithole, J. Chinamano and Shamuyarira, all representing ZAPU; Mushonga and L. Chiota, appearing for the Pan-African Socialist Union. There was also an independent multiracial group which included Josia Gondo. Both ZAPU and PASU pointed to the discrimination obtaining in Rhodesia, rejected the 1961 Constitution and urged Britain to call a constitutional conference. The multiracial group confined itself to an appeal to the United Nations to help establish a nonracial society and not to encourage those who sought to excite racial passions in order to achieve their own political ambitions.

On behalf of the Afro-Asian states, Togo then submitted a draft resolution calling (1) for the release of African nationalists, (2) and for the lifting of the ban on ZAPU. Finally, it asked Britain to inform the General Assembly on the implementation of this very resolution. By 83 votes to 2, with 11 abstentions, the Assembly adopted this resolution on October 12, 1962—Resolution 1755 (XVII).

The voting pattern would persist, with some minor variations, in future resolutions on Rhodesia. Those in favor included the Afro-Asian and the Socialist states. On issues regarding liquidation of imperialism, colonialism and neo-colonialism, these two groups invariably agree, though not necessarily for the same reasons. Those against were Portugal and South Africa, Rhodesia's neighbors and partners in the white bastion against African rule. The abstainers included a large number of the Latin American states for whom the whole question was removed from their usual interests. The United Kingdom was recorded in a special category—"present and not voting."

Another debate took place in the Fourth Committee between October 22 and 30 of the same year, 1962. Sixty members of the UN participated, and urged Britain to intervene in Rhodesia as she had done in other territories under her control. A new feature in this debate was the explanation given for British reluctance to intervene. Poland, Ghana, Hungary, the Soviet Union and Congo-Leopoldville all drew attention to the alliance of South Africa, the Central African Federation, Katanga, and Portugal which, they alleged, was backed by two hundred industrial corporations to preserve white supremacy and, through it, their huge profits.

For this debate Britain was represented by a Cabinet Minister, J. B. Goldber, Minister of State for Foreign Affairs, to stress the importance she attached to it. But his contribution to the discussion contained nothing new. Instead, he stressed that the United Nations had no competence in the matter and cited the safeguards in the 1961 Constitution. Even Sir Edgar

Whitehead, the Rhodesian Prime Minister who had earlier denied the UN's competence, now appeared in person as a member of the British delegation. On October 30, he made a statement before the Committee in which he explained that a genuine nonracial society would emerge in Rhodesia as discriminatory practices against Africans gradually disappeared. He declared that his party, the UFP, and his government were committed to bringing about this change, and added prophetically, "Those who know me realise that I have risked the whole of my political future with a predominantly white electorate in preaching this not only here today, but also over the last two years, wherever I go." (By the end of the year, Sir Edgar's "risk" was his political undoing as he was ousted by his electorate for being too pro-African.)

But the Afro-Asian states and their supporters were not convinced by Sir Edgar's sincerity and eloquence. On October 30, they introduced through Mauritania a draft resolution which was revised and adopted the following day by the General Assembly as Resolution 1760 (XVII). Apart from reaffirming past UN resolutions, this resolution urged Britain to suspend the 1961 Constitution, to abolish discriminatory practices and to convene a new constitutional conference. A new feature was the request to the Secretary-General "to lend his good offices to promote conciliation among the various sections of the population of Southern Rhodesia by initiating prompt discussions with the United Kingdom Government and other parties concerned." He was also asked to report to the General Assembly's current session on the implementation of the Declaration on Independence to Colonial Areas. The Secretary-General acted, but was informed by Britain in June, 1963, that because of her constitutional relationship with Rhodesia she could not comply with UN resolutions.

The October, 1962, debates marked the parting of the ways between Britain and the United Nations on the question of Rhodesia. The break was made more dramatic by the resignation of Sir Hugh Foot from the British delegation because Britain had not accepted his proposals on action in Rhodesia. Sir Hugh explained that he could no longer support a policy opposed to his beliefs. The deadlock between the United Nations and Britain had resulted from a basic difference of view. While the United Nations hammered away at Britain's responsibility, Britain felt that she was being pressed into actions far beyond her competence and rights. Future debates were to reflect the persistence of this difference of outlook.

The deadlock again appeared in the first debate by the Security Council in September, 1963. This was held at the insistence of some thirty African states whose view was that Rhodesia threatened peace and security. The threat lay in the heavily armed land and air units (especially the Royal Rhodesian Air Force) which, with the dissolution of the federation, would be handed over to Rhodesia. The African states feared that these would be used against the Africans in Rhodesia. Ghana, Morocco and the Philippines then introduced a draft resolution asking Britain not to transfer to Rhodesia these armed forces and other attributes of sovereignty. After denying the Council's competence, Britain argued that the armed forces were merely reverting to Rhodesia, and not being transferred. Ghana attacked this argument by pointing out that the forces were more powerful than those originally handed over to the federation by Rhodesia.

The United States view was that the Council should take no action, since the impending dissolution of the federation would not produce any deterioration of the situation in Rhodesia. France, while recognizing the significance of the problem for the African states, rejected the action proposed in the draft resolution because the United Kingdom's interests did not violate the Charter provisions on self-determination. The Soviet Union fully supported the resolution, since it contained the minimum African demands. Brazil, China, Venezuela and Norway indicated their support. On September 13 voting showed 8 in favor, 1 against, and 2 abstentions, the United States and France. Since the negative vote had been passed by a permanent member of the Council, Britain, and therefore constituted a veto, the resolution could not be adopted. This was the first British veto since the Suez crisis in 1956.

Following the dissolution of the federation, Britain and Rhodesia could not reach agreement on independence. Therefore, the threat of a unilateral declaration of independence by Rhodesia came increasingly to the fore, and somewhat softened the attitude of Britain toward the United Nations on the question of Rhodesia. In a debate in the Special Committee, March, 1964, Britain, while still maintaining that the United Nations had no competence, nevertheless informed the Committee of recent negotiations with the Rhodesian government. She pointed out that these were difficult and delicate and required care and patience. Many members sought a categorical assurance that Britain would not grant independence to Rhodesia under minority rule, and urged her to make clear to the Field regime the grave consequences of UDI and to convene a constitutional conference. Italy and the United States suggested a preliminary conference. On none of these points did the United Kingdom give immediate satisfaction. However, the Subcommittee reported in April, after a visit to London, that Britain had expressed to Rhodesia her disapproval of UDI and had said that she favored a widening of the franchise before independence. But the Subcommittee regretted that Britain had not indicated the measures she would take to oppose UDI.

In October, the Special Committee received a more satisfactory reaction from Britain. Her delegation read a statement issued on October 27 by the British Prime Minister that UDI "would have no constitutional effect. The only way in which Rhodesia can become a sovereign independent state is by an act of the British Parliament. A declaration of independence would be an open act of defiance and rebellion and it would be treasonable to take steps to give effect to it."[1] The British delegation also added that their government favored a peaceful transition to majority rule. The Committee welcomed this stand by Britain and refrained from passing resolutions in the Assembly or the Security Council.

For the Organization of African Unity (OAU), 1965 brought a deterioration in Rhodesia. The OAU, therefore, asked the Foreign Ministers of Algeria and Senegal to request a meeting of the Security Council. This took place from April 30 to May 6. Foreign Minister Thiam of Senegal opened the debate by accusing Britain of dereliction of duty toward the Africans of Rhodesia by taking no positive steps at all. These she could now take by suspending the snap election scheduled for May 7, which Mr. Smith was holding to obtain a two-thirds majority and a mandate for UDI. The United Kingdom was also urged to secure the release of all detainees, annul the 1961 Constitution and call for a conference. He warned that the African states would not sit idly by if Britain took no action. The Algerian Minister, Bouteflika, emphasized that the situation required preventive, not remedial, steps and called for immediate action.

For the United Kingdom, Lord Caradon, the former Sir Hugh Foot, who had resigned in 1962, stated that the policy of the new Labour government rested on three principles: (1) independence would be granted only on a basis acceptable to all the people of Rhodesia, (2) the solution to the problem had to be sought by negotiation, not by illegal action, and (3) nobody should doubt the true constitutional position or political and economic consequences of UDI. As for the impending election, this was an internal Rhodesian matter beyond the competence of Britain. Thus in the attitude of Wilson's Labour government there was no essential departure from the Conservative line, and this bipartisan approach lasted right up to the fateful November 11. The only departure from the Conservatives was the clear commitment of Labour to negotiation as the way to a solution. Labour soon showed that she meant abjuring the use of force even in the event of UDI, whereas the Conservatives had strengthened their hand in negotiation by retaining the possible use of force as a deterrent to an illegal declaration. Since the Labour government had been elected by a very slim majority, three votes, it could ill afford taking a tough line toward Rhodesia for fear of alienating the Conservatives and right-leaning Labour members who together could have toppled Wilson.

For the Soviet Union, Ambassador N. Fedorenko put the blame squarely on the shoulders of Britain, the responsible power. He returned to the theme that Britain was a party to the Unholy Alliance in southern Africa through the interlocking system of industrialists and capitalists with vested interests in the maintenance of exploitive rule. As regards Lord Caradon's address, Fedorenko noted a sad metamorphosis in the convictions of the man who had earlier resigned over the very same policy he was now advocating. In his defense, Lord Caradon denied the metamorphosis, and referred Fedorenko to his book.[2] Ironically noting that since for the Soviet Union even buying the book would be too much of a voluntary contribution to make, he offered Fedorenko a copy on the spot!

Ambassador Usher, of the Ivory Coast, then submitted a draft resolution which he rather sadly admitted was a compromise. This had been done, he said, to ensure its speedy adoption by the Council so as to meet the grave situation in Rhodesia. The resolution took note of the British statement of October 27, 1964, and urged Britain to convene a constitutional conference to prevent UDI and not to transfer any powers or attributes of sovereignty to Rhodesia's minority government.

While Ambassador Adlai Stevenson for the United States shared the Africans' fears and expressed disappointment at Smith's repressive rule, Fedorenko dismissed the draft resolution as flabby and inadequate to meet the requirements of the explosive situation obtaining in Rhodesia. He scored the apologetic tone of the draft—its stress on requests. Further, it said nothing about stopping the election or abrogating the 1961 Constitution. Since, he declared, the Soviet Union stood on the principle of the immediate liquidation of colonialism, he was therefore strengthening the draft by amending it. The Soviet amendments were rejected, with the United States and Britain voting against. There were eight abstentions.

On May 6 the African draft resolution was voted upon as Resolution 202. The voting was: seven in favor, none against. But the four Big Powers and strongest members of the UN—United States, Soviet Union, France and Britain—all abstained, thus depriving the resolution of whatever semblance of powerful support it might otherwise have had. This was a bitter blow to the OAU, and for Rhodesia a victory without a fight. Why did this happen? Both France and Britain explained immediately after the voting that they still had reservations on the United Nations' competence. The Soviet Union maintained that the resolution was inadequate. The United States regarded the resolution as constructive but unbalanced. The demands in it could not be implemented by Britain alone without the cooperation of the Rhodesian authorities. Therefore, she had abstained.

Future researchers may well discover that one factor greatly influenced the voting behavior of certain delegations in this debate. Apart from the Soviet Union, most members of the Council had been impressed by the reasonable approach of the OAU-sponsored resolution. Then the US Marines landed in Santo Domingo and the picture changed. Before the landing, many African delegates privately and confidently predicted in the Delegates' Lounge the Security Council's acceptance of the resolution, since they had sounded out their colleagues from other areas. Then, suddenly, Santo Domingo injected a new and disruptive note—with some delegations agreeing to support the resolution only if the Africans in turn gave help on this thorny problem. The fact that all the Big Four abstained suggests that the Africans held back.

In his final comments, Ambassador Usher warned that the Rhodesian situation could not be summed up in tidy legal formulas of competence in some spheres and incompetence in others. What Usher in effect was saying was that the Rhodesian problem went far beyond jurisdictional bounds. The law of the jungle reigned in Rhodesia and threatened to culminate in UDI. Therefore, power politics was necessary to meet this threat. There was, however, no change in the stand of those Western states alone capable of forcing Premier Smith to mend his ways.

The United Nations debates show all the powerful permanent members, except the Soviet Union, lining up behind Britain. To account for this unity of the Western stand on Rhodesia, one does not have to be a dogmatic believer in the conspiracy theory of politics and history. Policy statements alone throw sufficient light on the matter. The address[3] on December 19, 1965, by the US Assistant Secretary of State for African Affairs, G. Mennen Williams, makes the point lucidly enough.

Speaking to the American Legion after UDI, the Assistant Secretary plainly stated that the rebellion was of direct concern to the United States not only because of the American belief in equality and democracy but also because of the critical consequences that could be unleashed all over Africa if the rebellion were not ended quickly. One of these would be that Britain, the closest ally of the US, would lose her influence in Africa and her power in the rest of the world. Failure to quell the rebellion would also seriously endanger the entire US policy in Africa. "The simple fact is that our entire posture in Africa rests squarely on the strong moral and material support we give African nations on issues of vital importance to them. . . ."

He condemned UDI and the repressive measures of Smith in the strongest terms. Mr. Williams then considered the means to be used to topple the Salisbury regime. He found the extensive British sanctions dependent for their effectiveness on three intangibles: (1) the amount of cooperation between

South Africa and Rhodesia to break the sanctions, (2) "the predatory tendencies of modern-day private buccaneers looking for quick profit" and (3) the amount of patience and restraint by the African states. The first two are the crux of the whole matter, and one would have expected the United States to take her own steps to tackle them so as to ensure the success of the British effort with sanctions. One way would have been to impose mandatory sanctions on US corporations trading with Rhodesia. Instead, while fully backing Britain, the United States merely requested US corporations to stop trading. Some defiantly went on.

Three months after UDI, US tobacco purchases were reported to be worth $190,000; the corporations, United Carbide and Vanadium Corporation, continued importing chromite. The American Committee on Africa commented, "The American government's halfhearted attempt to back economic sanctions against Ian Smith's Rhodesian autocracy shows us still stubbornly resolved to ignore the danger."[4] A likely reason for this halfhearted attempt may well lie in the difference of opinion which, according to David Willis,[5] existed among US policy makers. Some officials favored direct action by the United States; others stood for US support of Britain. At any rate, both the forays of the buccaneers and the division among the officials made for uncertain and ineffective policy. This was reflected in the United States stand at the United Nations.

Immediate after UDI, Britain made a quick reversal of attitude toward the United Nations. Whereas she had never asked for meetings of the Security Council because she considered Rhodesia beyond the organization's jurisdiction, she now requested an urgent meeting. The Foreign Secretary, Michael

Stewart, came in person to present his government's case. This rested on the premise that selective economic sanctions would topple the rebel regime in Salisbury. Although the Afro-Asian members were skeptical and wanted more stringent measures to be used, including force, the British view prevailed, and the Council adopted Resolution 216 by 10 votes in favor, 0 against and 1 abstention, France. This resolution condemned UDI and called upon all states not to recognize "this illegal racist minority regime in Southern Rhodesia and to refrain from rendering any assistance to this illegal regime."

Further, on November 2, 1965, and by the same voting pattern, it adopted another resolution (217) which called upon Britain to quell the rebellion by taking "all other appropriate measures which would prove effective in eliminating the authority of the usurpers." All states were also asked "to do their utmost in order to break all economic relations with Southern Rhodesia, including an embargo on oil and petroleum products." The second resolution was voted upon by Britain herself because it excluded the use of force—in keeping with the principles which Lord Caradon had propounded before the Council in April and Prime Minister Wilson in October. While maintaining that the resolution did not go far enough, the Soviet Union nonetheless voted for it. (Whereas in the previous May, the Soviet Union had abstained because the resolution was inadequate.)

A change of roles then fell upon the Ivory Coast delegate, Ambassador Usher, who had submitted a compromise resolution in May. This time, he proposed on behalf of the OAU that the Council take firm action. He urged the Council to set up a UN military force to end the rebellion, and to take against the Smith regime all measures contained in Chapter

VII of the Charter. This deals with military and nonmilitary action. The British position was that the nonmilitary measures she proposed to take were enough to bring the rebels to heel. Thus, there existed a serious difference of view between the OAU and Britain on the most appropriate action to be taken. It fell to the Netherlands' chief delegate, Dr. J. G. de Beus, to suggest a compromise.[6] He warned that military action would unleash a disastrous war; but the British measures would be effective only if they had wide support. (Perhaps unwittingly, the Netherlands delegate saw in the British economic sanctions a flaw which South Africa and Portugal were to exploit in order to prop the rebel regime.) He therefore urged the Council to concentrate on those points on which all members agreed. In the end, the African draft resolution lost.

In a note of November 29, 1965, the Secretary-General transmitted the text of Resolution 217 to member states, and drew their attention to those sections pertaining to nonrecognition of the rebel regime and to withholding aid. Portugal and South Africa did not comply with this resolution because they held that the rebellion was a matter between Britain and Rhodesia alone. As Rhodesia's neighbors, they would continue to maintain normal relations.

The nonpolitical organs of the United Nations also acted against the rebel regime in Salisbury. On November 19, 1965, the Governing Council of the International Labor Organization (ILO) passed a resolution informing the Secretary-General of the United Nations that the ILO would take such action within its sphere as the Security Council deemed necessary. On the same day, the General Agreement on Tariffs and Trade announced that it had severed all relations with the rebels although Rhodesia would remain a member. At

Britain's request, the Food and Agriculture Organization (FAO) stopped considering Rhodesia's application for associate membership, while the United Nations Educational, Scientific and Cultural Organization (UNESCO) suspended communications. In short, Rhodesia was isolated from the councils of nations—a relatively small price for her to pay if she ultimately won.

The handling of the Rhodesian question by the UN throws some light on the strategy followed by the African states. Many of them realized their economic and military incapacity to crush the rebels by their own efforts and their inability to impose their will on the permanent members of the Security Council, China excluded. They, therefore, devised the strategy of a weak man with a strong case: to strike a pose of righteous anger accompanied by fiery speeches while applying pressure behind the scenes upon the United States and Britain. The various meetings in the UN organs were merely means of keeping the issue alive, providing Nkomo, Sithole and other nationalists and the OAU with a ready platform for Ciceronian oratory. However, in terms of actually changing the situation in Rhodesia, it was an exercise in futility. The same futility was evident in the deliberations of the Organization of African Unity.

CHAPTER TEN

AFRICA VERSUS WHITE RHODESIA

Joint African efforts on behalf of African nationalism in Rhodesia have consistently focused attention on the United Kingdom. The result has been a narrow and blurred view of the situation. Instead of dealing with Rhodesia as a problem challenging independent Africa because of the concentration in Rhodesia and the rest of southern Africa of a powerful and intransigent minority dominating an African majority, the solution to the Rhodesian problem was sought at No. 10 Downing Street. Pressures have been directed toward Britain and demands made for using military force to bring about a change.

Yet it is clear that Britain is in no position to act as demanded. Legally she may claim to be the sovereign; but the political fact is that since the occupation of Rhodesia in 1890, the initiative in Rhodesia has always been with the settlers. All Britain has had to do is to approve or, very rarely, to reject legislative or diplomatic proposals from successive settler governments.

Before the Organization of African Unity (OAU) confronted the Rhodesian situation in 1963, the attention of the continent and the international community was already caught by the activities of Rhodesian nationalists. This came about in the prior decade by the growing involvement of Rhodesians in Pan-African meetings. Most of the effort to publicize the Rhodesian problem was made by Joshua Nkomo, President of the ANC of Rhodesia. In the conferences of the Independent African States and the All African Peoples Organization, both held in Accra in 1958, he made the cause of his people known to English- and French-speaking Africa.

Meanwhile, between conferences, the Pan-African Freedom Movement of East and Central Africa (PAFMECA) was established in September 1958 with headquarters in Dar es Salaam, and under the leadership of Julius Nyerere of Tanganyika and Tom Mboya of Kenya. The main aim was to intensify the nonviolent struggle against colonialism and racialism. This it was to do by coordinating the nationalist programs and by establishing a joint Freedom Fund.[1] In the beginning PAFMECA confined its activities to East and Central Africa; but in February, 1962, it included nationalist movements in Rhodesia and other parts of southern Africa—hence the change of the name to PAFMECSA.[2] PAFMECSA and the two conferences held in Accra in 1958 enabled Nkomo to state his case in African capitals, in London and at the United Nations.

Under pressure by the increasing membership of Afro-Asian states, the UN first discussed Rhodesia in 1961 despite strong British protest that this was a domestic matter, beyond the UN's competence. In October there came, as petitioners, from ZAPU, Enoch Dumbutshena, the clergymen Ndabaningi Sithole and Michael Scott, and Nathan Shamuyarira, a former editor-in-chief of *African Newspapers,* a European-owned company which published newspapers for Africans. From the Pan-African Socialist Union of Zimbabwe (PASU)—formed as a protest against Nkomo's leadership of ZAPU—came Paul Mushonga, Phineas Sithole and Lucas Chiota. There were also five members of an "independent, multiracial group of Rhodesian citizens," among them J. M. Gondo. On October 31, both the Trusteeship Council and the General Assembly passed a resolution (with South Africa and Portugal voting against it) which called on Britain to suspend the 1961 Constitution and to cancel the elections due to be held under it. The resolution was not carried out.

Against this background, the OAU intensified the struggle by putting more pressure on Britain in the form of strong resolutions, threats, extensive publicity in the various organs of United Nations and in the meetings of the Commonwealth Prime Ministers. These OAU efforts have commanded greater attention than those of PAFMECSA because as an organization of states, the OAU had more prestige.

At the inaugural meeting of the OAU Conference of the Heads of States in Addis Ababa (May 22–25, 1963), the liberation of the whole continent was the prime concern of the

Heads of State. This feeling can be gauged from the fiery remark attributed to Ben Bella: "I do not give a scrap for your Charters. What concerns me is the sincerity of this conference towards the final Liberation of Africa."[3] In his moving opening address, Emperor Haile Selassie also said: "Our liberty is meaningless unless all Africans are free. Our brothers in the Rhodesias, Mozambique, and Angola, as well as in South Africa, cry out in anguish for our support and assistance. We must align and identify ourselves with all aspects of their struggle."[4]

In keeping with this spirit, the leaders of liberation movements and the representatives of nonindependent governments were given a special role at the Conference. They were asked to form an advisory committee to put forward their recommendations. For spokesman, they chose Oginga Odinga, head of the Kenya delegation, who presented a memorandum signed by representatives of twenty-one liberation movements, including the Zimbabwe African Peoples Union (ZAPU). The National Zimbabwe Party (NZP) of Patrick Matimba attended the Conference, but was not invited to sign the memorandum, since the other liberation movements regarded it as not representative of the people of Rhodesia.

The memorandum specifically mentions Rhodesia.[5] Point 6 urges the independent states to set up a committee to confer with leaders of liberation movements in Rhodesia and other countries so that they can form united fronts. Point 10 urges the same states to extend their economic and diplomatic boycott of South Africa to "the racist settler regime of Southern Rhodesia and the imperialist Britain." More important, however, was the recommendation that the OAU establish a Liberation Bureau to coordinate the struggle and distribute funds and military equipment. The Conference incorporated these suggestions in its resolution on decolonization, which asked Britain not to transfer power in Rhodesia to the minority government. Should this happen, however, then the OAU would give "effective moral and practical support to any legitimate measures which the African nationalist leaders may devise for the purpose of recovering such power and restoring it to the African majority."

In the same resolution, the Assembly fixed May 25 as African Liberation Day, and set up a nine-member Coordinating Committee to coordinate the assistance from the African states to liberation movements and to manage the Special Fund for liberation activities. Four points are worth noting about this Committee, more popularly known as the Liberation Committee or the Committee of Nine. First of all, Ghana, a country second to none in its dedication to liberating the continent, was not chosen. The members are Algeria, Ethiopia, Guinea, Congo (Leopoldville, now Kinshasa), Nigeria, Senegal, Tanzania, United Arab Republic, and Uganda.[6] Secondly, the Committee is a non-Charter organ of the OAU—created by an Assembly. In this way the African states emphasize, perhaps too optimistically, that liberation is a temporary phase on the road to continental unity. Thirdly, the Committee has its own independent budget (to which member states contribute voluntarily), and its own Secretariat with headquarters in Dar es Salaam. Both distance and financial independence tend to make the Committee independent of control by the Administrative Secretary of the OAU in Addis Ababa, a development which has displeased some members and made them reluctant to finance a body over which they have little firm control. Lastly, the Committee replaced PAFMECSA which was dissolved in September 24, 1963.

Soon after its foundation, the fledgling Liberation Committee was faced with a severe test when the ranks of ZAPU split asunder in July and August, 1963. The break was not unexpected. Since 1961, when Nkomo first accepted, then rejected, the Constitution, growing dissatisfaction with his leadership had led to the foundation of NZP and PASU. These two, however, never had much of a following. But the 1963 split was more serious because it was led by some of Nkomo's own close colleagues in the ZAPU Executive, who on August 8 formed themselves into the Zimbabwe African National Union (ZANU). These were Reverend Ndabaningi Sithole, Robert Mugabe, Leopold Takawira and Booker T. Washington Malianga. They were joined by Advocate Herbert Chitepo and Nathan Shamuyarira, who has given his version of the split in his book, *Crisis in Rhodesia.*[7]

An important factor in this split was the opposition of some African leaders outside Rhodesia to Nkomo's concentration on international contacts rather than on the struggle at home. While they regretted the split, they gave ZANU moral support and hoped that because of its dynamic program it would quickly supersede ZAPU inside Rhodesia. This has not yet happened. Instead, the African states themselves are now divided, some favoring ZAPU, others ZANU. A brief line-up of some key states showed the following in May, 1966:

State	*Group Favored*
Algeria	ZAPU
United Arab Republic	"
Zambia	"
Ghana	ZANU
Malawi	"
Tanzania	"

Except for Malawi and Ghana, all these states are members of the Liberation Committee. The Committee's failure to bring about a reconciliation between ZANU and ZAPU is partly due to this division among its members. Indeed, in December, 1963, the Committee decided to recognize both groups and to allot funds to them.

Between June and August, 1965, the OAU Council of Ministers embarked on a campaign to reconcile the two groups because, as the periodical *West Africa* put it on October 16, "without the establishment of this unity the prospect of African rule is slender." A little earlier, in August, the pro-Nkrumah *Africa and the World,*[8] in a major article by the editor, Douglas Rogers, had urged that the OAU or, if that was impossible, some militant member states should organize a conference of all southern African liberation movements in order to iron out their differences and form a united front.

But such an OAU attempt had recently ended in failure. In keeping with Resolution 8 (1) of the 1964 Cairo Assembly, a subcommittee of the Liberation Committee—consisting of Malawi, Tanzania and the UAR—met the two groups in Lusaka in August, 1964, but failed to bring them together in a united common front.

In a Special Resolution on Southern Rhodesia (Resolution 9), passed at its Fifth Extraordinary Session held in Lagos, June 10–13, 1965, the Council went on record as deeply disturbed by the gulf between ZANU and ZAPU and by "their refusal, despite all attempts by the Organization of Unity, . . . to form a common front against the present Salisbury regime." A subcommittee of ministers was to recommend to the coming Accra Assembly of Heads of States ways of ending the split. The subcommittee decided to recommend the withdrawal of OAU funds from both ZAPU and ZANU if they failed to form a common front. They failed to unite, but the funds kept coming.

The responsibility for the failure lies with both groups. On June 15 the ZAPU Treasurer-General, Jason Moyo, rejected the call of the OAU Council on the grounds that his organization enjoyed popular support at home while ZANU, he alleged, was but a minor splinter group.[9] Sometimes ZAPU completely denied the existence of a split. As Shamuyarira rightly sums it up, Nkomo has argued that ZANU has "never had any support worth talking about; therefore unity with such a party was pointless. It would be just an admission of the existence of the non-existent."[10] Even the OAU threat of no funds has failed to change the ZAPU attitude because ZAPU, like ZANU, knows that it can easily receive money directly from African governments and others sympathetic to it.

But according to *The Reporter* of Nairobi,[11] both groups uncompromisingly stated terms unacceptable to the other at the secret reconciliation talks held in Nairobi under the auspices of the OAU Council. Led by Simpson Mtambanengwe, its Director of External Affairs, ZANU said that it was prepared to merge with ZAPU provided Nkomo was dismissed as leader. For its part, the ZAPU delegation, led by its General Secretary, George Nyandoro, stated that the only acceptable basis for discussion was that ZANU should immediately dissolve and return to the ZAPU fold under the leadership of Nkomo.

Whether the OAU was correct in devoting so much of its time and meager resources to bringing about a reconciliation is a subject of bitter, emotional and endless debate. Briefly put, the case for the OAU attempt is based on the fear that without a unified African opposition the present rulers in Rhodesia are assured of a long and profitable reign. There is no argument with the OAU goal, just its realism. A ZAPU-ZANU reconciliation was out of reach at that time and its pursuit, unrealistic. The OAU was reluctant to choose between the two rival organizations, but, in our view, political realism demanded such a choice, despite the fear of rival governments-in-exile and of support from outside the OAU. (In the case of Angola, this did not deter the OAU from recognizing Holden Roberto's group.) As a result of indecision, the OAU had to divide its attention between bringing about a reconciliation and making preparations to meet the impending UDI.

What strategy has the OAU followed, and with what results? In our view, the OAU has not quite seen the Rhodesian question within the context of a common determination among the governments of southern Africa to resist, at all cost, a change-over to African rule. The governments of Salazar, Smith and Dr. Verwoerd have helped each other defy African opinion and that of the Big Powers. According to *Spotlight on South Africa,*[12] Prime Minister Smith told a Portuguese journalist in April, 1965, that the governments of southern Africa should work together to "halt the threat of Communist-inspired Black nationalism."

Instead of seeing Rhodesia as an integral part of the so-called Unholy Alliance, the OAU has paid more attention to persuading Britain—as if, in this case, moral considerations rather than her own interests would convince Britain to act on behalf of the African population. Repeatedly, Britain has been told that to be consistent in her colonial policy, she must treat Rhodesia the same way as other African areas which she granted independence under majority rule. It has also been said that Britain has both the legal and military capacity to impose this solution in case the Rhodesian government resists. Whatever the merits of these arguments in theory, in practice successive Rhodesian governments have always enjoyed extraordinary latitude of power. The initiative for policies at home and abroad has almost invariably come from the Rhodesian government, with the British government merely approving or, very rarely, rejecting any proposals put to it. An examination of the resolutions passed and the steps taken by the OAU show this preoccupation with Britain as if she held the key to the solution.

The Council of Ministers specifically treated Rhodesia in its second ordinary session in Lagos, February 24–29, 1964. Resolution 14, based partly on a memorandum submitted by the ZAPU representatives G. Nyandoro and T. Silundika, calls on Britain to prevent UDI and to "Convene, without any further delay, a fully representative Constitutional Conference of all political parties in Southern Rhodesia to decide on the granting of immediate independence to Southern Rhodesia on the basis of 'one man, one vote.' " Should she fail to do so, then the Ministers recommended that the members of the OAU "reconsider their diplomatic and other relations" with her. The African Group at the United Nations was requested by the Ministers to "take appropriate diplomatic measures to ensure that the British Government implement, without delay, past United Nations resolutions on Southern Rhodesia."

Only one of the four paragraphs in the resolution calls on the Liberation Committee to strengthen its support of the African nationalists so that they may intensify their struggle for freedom. The difference in the amount of attention given to Britain and to the nationalists is typical of the whole OAU approach up to June, 1965, with its focus on constitutional change, diplomatic measures, persuasion. In July, 1964, the Council took essentially the same stand in Cairo. Despite the peaceful approach of the OAU, neither Britain nor the government of Rhodesia changed its course. Instead, there were clear signs of a deterioration.

However, from June, 1965, the OAU concentrated more on Rhodesia than on Britain. The Special Resolution on Southern Rhodesia (Resolution 9), passed at the Fifth Extraordinary Session of the Council held in Lagos, showed the OAU's deep concern over the division between ZAPU and ZANU. Although the General Resolution on Southern Rhodesia (Resolution 10) again calls upon Britain to convene a constitutional conference, this time the language is sharply critical of Britain, an indication of independent OAU action in Accra during the meeting of the Heads of State, October 21–25, 1965. After deploring Britain's refusal to deal firmly with the UDI, the Assembly resolved (Resolution 25) not only to reconsider all its relations with Britain but also "to use all possible means including force to oppose a unilateral declaration of independence." They promised to "give immediate assistance to the people of Zimbabwe with a view to establishing a majority government in the country."

Another resolution, passed in great secrecy, was later disclosed in Addis Ababa.[13] It set up a "watchdog" committee consisting of Kenya, Nigeria, Tanzania, United Arab Republic and Zambia to keep in touch with developments in Rhodesia and to undertake contingency planning in case of UDI. A clue to the resolution's content was evident in a resolution submitted in November by the Ivory Coast delegation to the

Security Council. This showed that the OAU aimed at a total trade embargo on Rhodesia, military intervention and, following the toppling of the Smith Government, immediate universal franchise.

Which states supported the use of force and economic sanctions? Statements after the Accra Assembly indicate that in addition to the "radicals" like Ghana, Guinea and Mali, "moderates" like Ethiopia, Nigeria, Senegal and Mauritania were among the proponents. But Rhodesia's immediate African neighbors, Malawi and Zambia, opposed these ideas because of their dependence on Rhodesia's electricity and railways.[14] Dr. Bauda also argued that since the Rhodesian Air Force could easily flatten every city in Central Africa, military intervention was a ridiculous proposition.

Prime Minister Ian Smith in an interview with Peter Enahoro, a Nigerian journalist, also discounted the threat of OAU intervention. The following exchange took place.

Enahoro: Do you think there is any danger of the OAU coming into armed conflict with your troops?

Smith: No, I don't believe so, certainly not even a vague possibility. I don't believe this is a possibility. I see no reason for it as long as we don't interfere in other people's affairs.[15]

The real reason for his confidence was not that Rhodesia was not interfering in "other people's affairs," but that if they did in hers, she was militarily prepared and able to inflict severe damage on an invader with her modern military equipment, especially in the Air Force. Although her troops are relatively few in numbers, there were unconfirmed (and undenied) reports that she had enlisted mercenaries. The Dutch daily, the *Nieuwe Rotterdamse Courant,* of Rotterdam,[16] quotes a West German source as saying that a group of mercenaries in civilian dress and under a German officer had already arrived in Rhodesia. The officer, Major Müller, said that "there was danger of a 'sabotage war' from Africans in Rhodesia and from those infiltrating from other countries."

By "sabotage war" or unconventional warfare, the officer ruled out a direct confrontation between the Rhodesian and the OAU forces. The latter have a formidable total of 492,500 regular troops, 515 combat aircraft and some 160 transport aircraft, but a combined effort involves immense logistical problems, especially in regard to transport, since none of the Big Powers was prepared to assist.[17] For this reason *Newsweek* remarked that "the clamorous calls to arms emanating from African capitals sounded more like bluster than an immediate threat."[18]

Another handicap stems from the decision-making machinery of the OAU itself. It is cumbersome and hinders swift action in cases of emergency. For the organization to send troops to Rhodesia, the Council of Ministers—if they meet to consider the matter—can only recommend to the Assembly. Then all the Heads must meet for the final decision. The majority of them jealously guard the sovereignty they enjoy under the present structure of the OAU and hesitate to hand effective power to an executive organ.

After UDI, Oscar Kambona of Tanzania delivered an impassioned speech to the newly created Defence Committee of Five, meeting in Dar es Salaam in November, declaring:

> Ian Smith and his cohorts are not talking—they are deploying troops and terrorising our brothers. Let us also deploy Africa's great might to rescue our brothers in Southern Rhodesia. Let us

mobilize all of Africa's resources to bring majority rule in Rhodesia. . . .

Let us sit down to spell out concrete action. This is what the Heads of State and Government have mandated us to do, and I am sure we shall not fail them.[19]

This speech amounts to an admission that the OAU never made any serious contingency plans for UDI. Even the Watchdog Committee set up in Accra obviously never came up with concrete proposals. This means that the threat of military intervention contained in the African resolution before the Security Council in November, 1965, was not backed up by a plan of action. It is clear, then, that the war declared on Rhodesia by some African states was nothing but a flurry of words.

The lack of planning necessitated the holding of an emergency meeting of the Council of Ministers in Addis Ababa from December 3 to 5, 1965, in order to give Britain a last chance to act in Rhodesia. On December 3, the Council issued an ultimatum saying that the OAU members would sever all relations with Britain if by December 15 she had not ended the illegal rule of Mr. Smith.

This decision has been questioned and condemned in Africa and elsewhere. Britain was given only twelve days to act, far too little time. It appears that the OAU saw the matter purely in terms of Rhodesia standing alone in defiance of Britain; thus, in their view, twelve days were enough. But Rhodesia is not alone; she is an integral part of the southern African complex which is battling the "winds of change." Therefore, as *The New York Times* rightly commented, "It would take a miracle to 'crush' the white rebel regime in Salisbury by December 15 with the means available to the

British Government."[20] The OAU ultimatum reveals a narrow view of the problems involved.

Another sound criticism came from *West Africa* which said: "By applying this ultimate sanction so soon, African states have not only thrown away a most valuable asset, but have opened the way to serious division in their own ranks."[21] This division was soon reflected in the reaction of individual Heads of State. President Yameogo of Upper Volta said that the Council has no authority to take decisions that bind on the OAU. All it can legally do is recommend to the Assembly. Some Ministers, however, felt that the Accra Resolution empowered them to act. But the uncertain legal status of the ultimatum could only be clarified by the Assembly itself.

Some disconcerting questions emerge. Is it possible that the various ministers came to Addis Ababa in December with no specific mandate and instructions from their own governments? The uncertain status of the ultimatum and the poor response to it suggest that the ministers acted without the knowledge of their chiefs. The other question is: Was it not possible for the ministers to communicate from Addis with their superiors back home before deciding on the ultimatum? If not, then the telephones and other means of quick communication necessary for diplomatic decision-making were not even available—a basic requirement for the realization of any Pan-African efforts.

The division mentioned by *West Africa* quickly appeared. Of the thirty-six OAU member states, only four broke off relations with Britain on December 15: Guinea, Niger, Senegal and Tanzania. Of these, Tanzania was the only Commonwealth member and the one with the most to lose economically. But she responded to the OAU's call because, in the words of President Nyerere, "we have no other alternative if we are to deserve the respect of the world and—more important—if we are to respect ourselves."[22] In his view, the OAU makes a laughingstock of itself if it does not implement its own resolutions. Despite an appeal by President Kaunda of Zambia that he reconsider his stand because it would endanger plans by Britain and the United States to airlift supplies for Zambia through Tanzania, Nyerere stood firm. He stood his ground even when advised to be cautious by Africa's elder statesmen, the Emperor Haile Salassie and President Kenyatta of Kenya.[23] Before the deadline, African diplomats at the United Nations expressed grave doubts that the threat would be carried out. Nyerere's militancy was, thus, a challenge to the OAU and by December 18, the countries in Group A had complied; those in Group B did not:

Group A	*Group B*
Algeria	Ethiopia
Ghana	Kenya
Guinea	Nigeria
Mali	Tunisia
Tanzania	Zambia
United Arab Republic	
Mauritania	
Congo (Brazzaville)	
Niger	
Senegal	

According to *The New York Times,* this grouping showed that the Rhodesian problem had "starkly exposed the division between African radicals and moderates and raised anew questions about the future effectiveness of the Organization of African Unity."[24] This labeling of certain states as "radicals"

(Group A) and "moderates" (Group B) is at best a rough guide to the position of these states on some issues. On others, there have been changes. Even on the Rhodesian one, these categories do not quite apply. If violent opposition to colonialism is one of the radicals' characteristics, then one would have expected all of them to break with Britain by the set date. But Ghana and the United Arab Republic wavered for some days instead of acting with alacrity, as did Niger, Senegal and Congo (Brazzaville), which are not usually referred to as radicals.

The moderates have been credited with sweet reasonableness and patience. Instead of resorting to "fiery resolutions or childish walkouts or bloody threats which cannot be made good,"[25] they tried to apply more pressure on Britain by convening a special meeting of the Security Council in December and of the Commonwealth Prime Ministers in Lagos in January 1966. Both of these produced no satisfactory results. In Lagos, "moderate" Sierra Leone took Britain to task for its inaction and demanded the immediate use of force,[26] while in the Security Council, Kenya urged that sanctions, economic or military, be imposed on Rhodesia under Chapter VII of the Charter. But apart from giving more publicity to the Rhodesian issue, these two meetings achieved nothing concrete.

Further division appeared in the Sixth Session of the Council of Ministers held in Addis Ababa from February 28 to March 5, 1966. The Council met to discuss measures to be taken to topple the illegal government in Salisbury and to help Zambia offset the economic difficulties resulting from UDI. The Council again felt that the ZANU-ZAPU split undermined whatever actions the OAU might take. Presidents

Nyerere and Kaunda were then appointed to reconcile the two groups. However, Algeria was reported to have argued unsuccessfully for the recognition of ZAPU as the only liberation movement enjoying popular support and to have urged that military intervention by the OAU must precede an uprising by the Africans in Rhodesia.[27] But before the Council could discuss positive steps to be taken, it split over the seating of a delegation representing the regime that had recently ousted President Nkrumah. Guinea, Mali and Tanzania withdrew from the meeting because the seating of the delegation meant that the Council no longer recognized Nkrumah. Kenya later withdrew because she disapproved of military coups which were "a serious menace to peace and stability in Africa."

On March 3, Tunisia submitted to the Council a draft resolution on Rhodesia. This contained a clause saying those states who had severed relations with Britain would be absolved of their promise to do so and might, if they wished, restore relations with Britain. The upshot was that Algeria, the United Arab Republic and Somalia withdrew, the Algerian reason being that the resolution showed the OAU's disavowal of all past action. The special clause, in the Algerian view, would make it impossible in the future for resolutions to bind all the members of the OAU.[28] In all, nearly a quarter of the OAU membership—eight—withdrew. These eight cannot all be classified as radicals. Kenya and Somalia were not among the radicals who broke off with Britain in December. This time they acted, but for different reasons. In short, the OAU was in disarray, a state of affairs expressed in its failure to act as a unit on the emotionally charged issue of liberating Rhodesia.

On balance, the main function of the OAU was to keep the

Rhodesian problem alive in international gatherings. The resulting attention and publicity to some extent restrained Britain in accommodating herself to the government of Mr. Smith. Without some African pressure through the OAU, Britain conceivably might have found a solution acceptable to the settler regime but not necessarily to the Africans. As already was the case, the Central African Federation (1953–1963) was imposed despite African opposition because it suited the white rulers of the Rhodesias and Nyasaland.

On the debit side, there is much to be criticized on the OAU's handling of the Rhodesian problem. The basic weakness has been to react to events in Rhodesia or in London rather than to act with initiative. This was caused by the very structure of the organization. Initiative means the ability to act quickly and decisively through a body that can decide on urgent matters and implement decisions speedily. As we pointed out, the Council does not have such power and the Assembly machinery is cumbersome.

Apart from structure, but related to it, is the policy which the OAU has pursued. It has been a policy of threats. The OAU thought that because it represents so many millions of people with potential wealth and power, it could threaten both Rhodesia and Britain. For such a policy to work, the threat must, above all, be credible. As Dean Acheson has put it, "A threat is not believed and therefore cannot deter, unless there is general conviction that the threatener has both the capacity and the intention to carry out the threat."[29]

Examined in the light of Acheson's views, the threats to invade Rhodesia and to sever relations with Britain appear empty indeed. The intention to invade was not supported by the capacity to do so. The Rhodesian government knows that lack of a base of operations near Rhodesia and of adequate transport rules out invasion unless one of the Big Powers gives a hand. Though not fully credible, the threat of invasion still has put Rhodesia on the alert. The consequence was well expressed by Nkrumah at the Cairo Assembly in July, 1964: "By raising a threat at Addis Ababa and not being able to take effective action against apartheid and colonialism, we have worsened the plight of our kinsmen in Angola, Mozambique, Southern Rhodesia and South Africa. We have frightened the imperialists sufficiently to strengthen their defenses and the repression in Southern Africa, but we have not frightened them enough to abandon apartheid supremacy to its ill-fated doom." In short, the threat of invasion worsened the position of the Africans in Rhodesia instead of improving it.

Moreover, the December 15 ultimatum for Britain lacked realism. It was impossible for Britain to deal with Rhodesia, South Africa and Portuguese Africa in twelve days, even if she wanted to. Secondly, in twelve days it would be impossible for those OAU members, especially those within the Commonwealth, to make alternative arrangements for their economies. This threat failed lamentably, since the members themselves refused by a large majority to carry it out. Instead of frightening Britain, the ultimatum backfired, causing division among OAU members and placing joint African action under a cloud. The United Nations fared no better.

CHAPTER ELEVEN

UDI AND THE RACE QUESTION

For the newly independent nations of Africa, the armed enemy camp of Rhodesia and the rest of white-subjugated Africa are constant reminders of lingering colonialism and an unfinished task. African leaders outdo each other in proclaiming determination to liberate their brothers in the South. They have threatened, bluffed and cajoled Britain and any of her Western allies whom they regard as slow to act against the Smith regime. Nor has Britain's close ally, the United States, emerged unscathed.

Yet the African appeal to end the minority rule in Rhodesia met with no response. In the United Nations, in the conferences of the Commonwealth Prime Ministers and in bilateral talks, those states capable of toppling the rebel regime hid behind the conveniently vague provisions of international law. In the absence of a true World Court, international law was invariably interpreted by the major Western powers—whose national interests did not coincide with the wishes of the Africans. As a result, the Salisbury regime became entrenched, and the African states were confronted with refusal by white nations to topple white tyranny. The recurrent issue of racialism appeared once again, this time in African reactions to UDI and its aftermath.

Race, in the popular sense of the term, has always been an element of Pan-Africanism. But on the whole this has been a conscious belief and pride in the unique "souls of black folk"—to use the title of Du Bois' book—whether these black folk are in the Americas, in Britain or in Africa itself. This consciousness has not sought to establish the superiority of the Africans over other peoples; this would be racialism. Colin Legum rightly makes this fine yet valid distinction between race-consciousness and racialism.[1] Though this distinction can be easily lost in the sound and fury of politics, it is noteworthy that racialism did not dominate African reactions to UDI.

Within Rhodesia itself, the African reaction to UDI is difficult to characterize, since the forces of "law and order" quickly snuffed out any open opposition. Arrests were made, marches broken up and shots fired. All these measures were in keeping with the government's UDI plan, revealed by ZAPU in a memorandum to the OAU Council of Ministers meeting in Accra in October 1965.[2]

In South Africa, too, silence reigned. Only the white parties outdid one another in rooting for Smith. Whatever African opinion there was can be gleaned from the banned African National Congress (ANC) and the Pan-African Congress (PAC). There, the denunciations were bitter, charging Britain with complicity in the deed and drawing constant attention to the economic stake of Britain in southern Africa. The charges cited the many business firms immersed in Rhodesia and striving for quick returns on investments. Therefore, it was alleged to be in the interests of such profiteers to prop up the Unholy Trio of Smith, Salazar and Verwoerd to ensure a steady flow of profits. A similar view is advanced by Rosalynde Ainslie in her pamphlet, *The Unholy Alliance.*[3] In short, the ANC stressed that interlocking economic interests determined British policy rather than a racial conspiracy on the part of the West. But though related, racism and profiteering are not the same.

Outside of southern Africa, reaction was quick. Ghana was the first African state to issue a fiery statement with accusations of racist and economic intrigues:

> To the Government of Ghana it seems clear that an international complex of financial interests which derive profits from the exploitation of the African people are actively engaged in supporting the treasonable and treacherous Smith regime and that unless the Commonwealth, the Security Council and the Organisation of African Unity act quickly to deal boldly with the Southern Rhodesian rebellion, no other solution would be effective and the southern part of Africa would pass into the hands of the most vicious racialists which have yet been seen.[4]

While other states were just as vehement, they did not stress racialism. Even usually moderate Liberia came out in favor of harsh measures to deal with the rebellion. On November 12, 1965, President Tubman told Parliament that he interpreted

Prime Minister Wilson's statement that Governor Gibbs would be protected to mean that Britain would use force. "If my conjecture is correct," he said, "then I agree with the position of the British Government. If my conjecture is wrong, then I join those who contend for harsher measures."[5] Despite the hedging, these are strong words, though free of racial animosity.

In a survey of reactions, John Hargreaves reports that although the rest of the English-speaking states in West Africa felt very strongly about UDI and Britain's role in it, he found no racial ill-feeling.[6] The same was true of the French-speaking states, though they could more easily afford to be intemperate, since they are less closely connected with Britain and do not have the practical reservations of Commonwealth members. The most prominent reactions revolved around invading Rhodesia. Thus Niger reacted by pointing out that if President de Gaulle could make a million French settlers see sense in Algeria, it should be easier for Britain to do the same with 220,000 in Rhodesia. In the then Congo-Leopoldville, Foreign Minister Cleophas Kamitatu urged the African states to take joint action.[7]

By far the most soundly argued presentation of African feeling on the Rhodesian question was made by President Nyerere of Tanzania. In *Foreign Affairs,* April, 1966, he explained African anger and impatience in order to allay the mutual suspicion between Africa and the Western world which was in danger of damaging their relationship. African wrath, he said, had a rational basis. The Smith rebellion "represents an attempt to expand the area, and strengthen the hold in Africa, of doctrines which are inimical to the whole future of freedom in this continent."[8] While these doctrines of colonialism and racialism continued to exist, none of the independent states of Africa could live in peace and dignity.

In a brilliant summary, he showed the operation of these reactionary forces in South Africa and the Portuguese-ruled territories of Mozambique and Angola. Together with Rhodesia, these regimes enjoyed the support of Western business and financial interests.

In view of the many ties and issues at stake, why did Nyerere and the whole OAU focus on Britain to bring about a change in Rhodesia? President Nyerere recounts a story of disillusionment. He explains that the African states hoped that Britain would act in accordance with her colonial policy of granting freedom with safeguards for all and advance Rhodesia along constitutional lines to majority rule, then independence. It was particularly hoped that Britain would do so once she realized the "seriousness of a situation in which Southern Rhodesia existed as an outpost of South Africa, but operated under the name and responsibility of the British Crown."[9]

To Africa, the sincerity and traditions of Britain and the whole Western world were on trial, for here was a case of injustice where something could be done. Like Professor Gwendolen Carter, Nyerere pointed out that Dr. Verwoerd, the Prime Minister of South Africa, had advised Mr. Smith against UDI as an illegal act. Professor Carter notes: "Verwoerd has always taken his stand on strict legality and insistence on national sovereignty. He believes that Ian Smith has broken the line on the legal issue and that, therefore, if he supports Smith, he is imperiling the argument he uses most strongly to prevent outside countries from interfering with South Africa."[10] Thus, Verwoerd could give open support to Smith only at the risk of inviting attack on South Africa—

hence the official neutrality but private sympathy and aid to the rebellious action. Portugal took the same stand as South Africa.

Africans were outraged that the Western countries knew of the help that Salazar and Verwoerd were funneling to Smith to cushion him against the adverse effects of the voluntary sanctions. African leaders then saw a way of dealing with the White Redoubt without acting illegally against either South Africa or Portugal. If sanctions were made mandatory on all United Nations members, then South Africa and Portugal would have to stop abetting the rebellion or face international rebuke. Since the UN would be dealing with Rhodesia, it would not be interfering in South African affairs. In African eyes, as Nyerere pointed out, legality and morality coincided on the Rhodesian issue. Yet, the West refused to impose mandatory sanctions. Was it because they realized that the defeat of Rhodesia would open the way to the downfall of Salazar and Verwoerd and to the loss of the lucrative profits they were reaping? This question gave rise to the growing suspicions and charges of insincerity. Nyerere concluded by saying that in their efforts to topple the Smith regime, the weak African states, disillusioned with the West, would turn to the East for allies and help. President Nyerere's case was watertight. It challenged the West on its own grounds, its own stated beliefs and traditions. To make it, he needed no appeal to racial feelings.

UDI also aroused anger among American Negroes, who thereby expressed their bond with Africans in their struggle against white domination. A group of Detroit Negroes wrote a letter to Henry Ford of Ford Motors, asking him "to sever whatever financial and economic ties your company has in

Rhodesia" because the country was being ruled by a white supremacist regime. After reminding Mr. Ford that many Negroes died in the Second World War in order to "bring an end to government dedicated to a similar superman concept," the group concluded: "We are sure that you, who served with honor and distinction in World War II, do not want to give assistance in any form to the perpetuation of another government which espouses principles akin to those we fought against."[11] The letter reached the company, but business continued as usual.

Among Civil Rights organizations, the National Urban League, through its Executive Director Whitney Young, sent a letter to UN Ambassador Arthur J. Goldberg. The Urban League denounced the racist policies of the Smith regime and urged the United States to apply the strongest possible sanctions. It further called upon the United States government to give full support to the British embargo and, more important, to adopt an independent position which would put the United States squarely on the 'side of the right,' and not place her simply in a supportive or "me-too" position. Such a stand, the Urban League contended, would demonstrate to the American Negro the sincere commitment of the United States to racial equality and strong opposition to white supremacy.[12]

The National Association for the Advancement of Colored People (NAACP) also came out in full support of strong action. On December 13, 1965, its Executive Committee passed a resolution, later sent to Ambassador Goldberg, which called for the "imposition of any sanction within our power, short of intervention by the armed forces of the United States." In the event that other states wanted to attack Rhodesia, the NAACP pointed out that there was a precedent in US practice and traditions for lending assistance to such states. The NAACP was apparently referring to possible action by the OAU, which would be in need of logistical and transportation assistance.

The NAACP condemned the rebellion as based "without pretence or apology, upon the perpetuation of naked racism," and urged the United States to have "no part in abetting the ugly business of racism." The resolution concluded: "The black and brown peoples of the world have provided too much evidence of the falseness of the inflammatory doctrine of white supremacy to sit idly by while it is used as a spur to racist demagogues across the world and as a vehicle to oppressive power."[13]

While condemning UDI, the United States government merely asked the corporations trading with Rhodesia to voluntarily stop trading. A few did comply; others went ahead with impunity. One cannot, therefore, fully credit the Negro interest groups with successfully pressuring their government. United States action apparently was determined more by considerations of British interests than by concern for the reactions of United States Negroes.

A bold view of the situation was made by the blunt, craggy fighter Charles P. Howard, a columnist for *Muhammad Speaks* and for the *Afro-American*. In the *Afro-American* of November 30, 1965, he accused three forces of abetting the Smith regime: the OAU for failing to create unity government in Accra in October, 1965; ZAPU and ZANU for dividing the Africans at home; and the African chiefs who supported Smith. He also called for joint OAU military action; otherwise, he warned, it would be impossible to cope with the "NATO-supplied-and-directed Rhodesian and South African force."

In the same newspaper on December 11, 1965, Howard

blamed the trouble in Rhodesia and in the rest of Africa upon the Western meddling in search for quick profits. The racialists of southern Africa, in his view, exist at the pleasure of the foreign financiers whose servants they are. In essence, Howard, Nkrumah and the ANC had the same outlook: racism in Africa will end only if the capitalists are deprived of their source of profit. In the end, both the racists and the profiteers will have to go.

First of all, many states, while abhorring the policies of Mr. Smith, have been deterred by the realization of their military and economic weakness. Of course, if present, rabid and fanatic racism would have blinded them to this essential fact. Several African states depend directly for whatever standard of living they enjoy on Britain or Rhodesia herself or on Commonwealth preferences; therefore, breaking all ties with Britain would be self-destructive. Further, African states realize that the Unholy Trio are armed with formidable NATO equipment with which they can devastate large areas of poorly armed Africa. Themselves weak, and knowing the influence of economic power, many states thus easily believed that British sanctions would bring the Smith regime to its knees. This is the realism of the weak, not the fanaticism of the mighty.

As long as Africa remains economically dependent on outside resources, she will remain politically weak. Directly flowing from economic weakness is what Pratt calls Africa's different style of politics. Among other things, this consists in "the taking of postures that express a hope rather than a reality, a momentary assertion of an idealism rather than a firm commitment."[14] Strictly speaking, this is not uniquely African. One can think of Western countries which denounce Communism, while going all out for the ruble; one can also think of Eastern countries that fulminate against apartheid, while at the same time plying a profitable, but clandestine trade with South Africa. Thus when the OAU decides on a course of action which members later ignore because it is not in their national interests, they are merely doing in public what other states do without fanfare. No doubt lack of experience in the techniques of diplomacy accounts for some of these blunders; so does acceptance by some states of roles as moderates and radicals. These politically tinged labels, in turn, make some states take simplistic views of others as "puppets" or troublemakers—*onrustokers* is the fitting Dutch term. Acceptance of such labels breeds suspicion and dissension, neither of which promotes the cause of liberating Rhodesia. Clearly the aftermath of UDI was more an exercise of prudence and rhetoric than a demonstration of African power.

CHAPTER TWELVE

A STATE BUT NOT A NATION

Born in anger, maintained by force, surrounded by crisis, Rhodesia passed the point of no return on November 11, 1965. It became a self-proclaimed state, and the longer that fact remained unchallenged, the harder it became to reverse the process. As W. M. Knox, chairman of the ruling Rhodesia Front Party, said on April 30, 1966: "Rhodesian independence is now a *fait accompli* and we can no more go back to the pre-November 11th era even if we wanted to than a man can turn himself back into a child."[1]

But neither could that self-styled state turn itself into a nation any more than a stepchild could be transformed into a true-born heir of his father's lands. In point of fact, Rhodesia is more state than nation, and on this distinction hangs the tale of law, toil and trouble.

Since Rhodesia is an actor on the international stage, the question of whether she is a state under international law is of central importance. If she is, then her domestic policies and the treatment meted out to her citizens are, strictly speaking, not relevant to her standing as an international entity. It is general practice for states to avoid involvement in the purely domestic policies of other states, however obnoxious such policies may be. Thus, although a number of countries disapprove of the internal policies and practices of the Soviet Union and the Republic of South Africa, this disapproval in no way affects the status of these countries under international law. Even when a particular state is not recognized by another, this does not detract from its international competence. The People's Republic of China is a case in point. To British criticism that nonrecognition of this state by the United States was unrealistic, Secretary of State, John Foster Dulles, replied in 1958:

> The question of recognition involves to some extent a play on words. There is no doubt that we recognize Communist China as a fact. . . . It's a fact and we deal with it as a fact, and whenever it is advantageous to the world or for peace to do business with it, we don't hesitate to do business with it.
>
> Then there is another form of recognition which means diplomatic recognition. That carries with it great advantages to the recognized state. It turns over assets throughout all the world to its control. It puts it in a position of prestige. . . .
>
> But we do not give it all the surplus advantage which would flow from general diplomatic recognition, because those added advan-

tages would merely be used against us and against all the things we believe in. So we think the practical policy of realism is to do that.[2]

What Secretary Dulles so authoritatively said of the United States policy toward China is briefly this: *de facto* recognition means that the facts of international life prevent the United States from ignoring a diplomatic reality. A similar judgment applies to Rhodesia. Britain failed to bring her to heel by enforcing her authority, while from November onward Rhodesia maintained her independence despite internal and external opposition. This leads to the conclusion that Rhodesia and her government constitute a state, *de facto*. In addition, two other states, Portugal and the Republic of South Africa, do treat her as such now.

The case for Rhodesia's independence gains more weight from a historical study of her international activities under British rule. All along she has exercised real, effective sovereignty, and Britain's control has been a legal fiction, maintained by Rhodesia for her own political convenience. It can be shown that Southern Rhodesia, even before federating with Northern Rhodesia and Nyasaland in 1953, already enjoyed an international status, particularly in the Commonwealth. To argue the point fully would take us far beyond this chapter, which deals less with legal matters and more with political ones. Suffice it to say that the longer Rhodesia's unilaterally declared independence lasts as a fact, the more difficult it will be for her opponents to deny her legal status.

But there remains the political question of Rhodesia as a nation-state. It is on this score that internal factors militate against her claim to be a true nation-state. In short, *she lacks the consciousness* of being a nation. Here the touchstone provided by John Stuart Mill in *Considerations on Representative Government* can be applied:

> A portion of mankind may be said to constitute a nationality, if they are united among themselves by common sympathies, which do not exist between them and any others—which make them cooperate with each other more willingly than with other people, desire to be under the same government, and desire that it should be government by themselves, or a portion of themselves, exclusivily.[3]

For a people to be a nation, Mill points out that they must have "common sympathies," especially "identity of political antecedents; the possession of a national history, and consequent community of recollections; collective pride and humiliation, pleasure and regret, connected with the same incidents in the past."[4] History's proper contribution to nationhood is that it anchors the present generation to its forerunners. UDI deprived Rhodesia of that anchor.

Ernest Renan throws additional light on the matter in his essay, "Que'st-ce qu'une nation?" (1887). He dismissed common language and ethnic ties as constituents of nationality, and instead advanced the following: "To have common glories in the past, a common will in the present, to have accomplished the same things together, to desire to do the same; these are the conditions essential for a people to exist."[5]

For Renan, then, the past, present and the future must be tied together by the desire of a people to work together. It is this desire, this will to work together, accompanied by action flowing from it, which is of central importance. As Mill put it in his inimitable style:

> . . . political institutions (however the proposition may be at times ignored) are the work of men; owe their origin and their

whole existence to human will. Men did not wake up one morning and find them sprung up. Neither do they resemble trees, which, once planted, "are aye growing" while men "are sleeping." In every stage of their existence they are made what they are by human voluntary agency.[6]

Rhodesian experience with the white adventurer, then settler, then ruler has been against such a voluntary growth. In the beginning, Cecil Rhodes tricked King Lobengula into giving away his lands, and this has never been forgotten by today's Africans, be they Mashona or Mandebele. Its memory still fires opposition to the settlers. Furthermore, after Rhodesia was settled in 1890 by Europeans of British and Boer stock, the Africans took up arms to regain their land. In 1893, 1896 and 1897 they fought, but lost to the superior firearms of the settlers. In demonstrating the involuntary acceptance of white rule, these conflicts also provided Rhodesians with heroes. For the Africans, it was King Lobengula; for the settlers, it was Major Allan Wilson, whose valor in the 1893 fight became legendary.[7] Clearly, history provided Rhodesians with a bitter and divisive past, at odds with the emergence of a common national consciousness.

Psychologically, Europeans and Africans in Rhodesia have different social values and norms. Whereas the Africans aim at a nonracial society with the government elected on the basis of "one man, one vote," the ruling party of the Europeans stands for limited racial contact and for participation in government on the basis of "merit." In practice, this means that only Africans have to prove themselves worthy of a share in government. Such a policy is clearly designed to perpetuate settler rule as *Dagbreek,* an Afrikaans Sunday newspaper, indicated with disarming candor: "In both countries [South Africa and

Rhodesia] the maintenance of white leadership is a cardinal issue."

These differing norms and values find well-defined expression in public institutions. The Europeans who settled in Rhodesia brought from South Africa their traditional authoritarian, paternalistic attitude toward the Africans, which has made a lasting imprint on race relations in Rhodesia. This is evident from the statement made in 1938 by the then Prime Minister of Southern Rhodesia, Sir Godfrey Huggins (now Lord Malvern):

> The European in this country can be likened to an island in a sea of black, with the artisan and the tradesman forming the shores and the professional class the highlands in the centre. Is the native to be allowed to erode the shores and gradually attack the highlands? To permit this would mean that the leaven of civilization would be removed from the country, and the black man would revert to a barbarism worse than before. . . .

Sir Godfrey, therefore, proposed the division of Rhodesia into black and white areas:

> In the black areas, natives should be allowed to rise to any position they are capable of and should be protected from white competition. Every step of the industrial and social pyramid must be open to him, excepting only—and always—the very top. In the white areas the native should be welcomed, but on the understanding that he merely assists and does not compete with the white man.[8]

Such a policy of separating black from white in all spheres except the economic is based on the fear that the Africans, vastly outnumbering the settlers, would in an integrated society swamp the Europeans—"erode the shores and gradually attack the highlands."

For the white man, separation was their only protection, in separate government, economic, educational and social institutions. This is why the December, 1962, election ended in victory for Mr. Winston Field's Rhodesian Front which, reflecting the outlook of the white farmers and artisans, "denounced concessions to the Africans and openly asserted the indispensability of white political control."[9] The Smith regime demonstrated similar aims. Consistently, the white rulers have made deliberate attempts to foster separate loyalties so that there is no truly uniform and unified judicial, administrative and educational network of institutions.

From the absence of national institutions it follows that there are no national leaders—that is, leaders chosen by all the citizens, leaders whose legitimacy is recognized by all. On the European side, the interests of this group become identified with the interests of the whole state, while Europeans are expected to sink their differences for the sake of their group. It is no wonder, then, that conformity is extolled. It is particularly strong among newer immigrants who want to "belong" by showing determination to preserve the Europeans' way of life. Of the difficulties of dissent, Miss Margery Perham, a veteran student of African affairs, has written:

> To oppose, within Rhodesia, this pervasive atmosphere demands rare qualities, foresight, a sense of justice and humanity, and an independent and courageous mind. It is seldom the latest arrival from equalitarian Britain who shows this courage; the outstanding men have mostly been from the families of earlier settlement, sometimes of missionary settlement.[10]

To the latter group belong people like Sir Robert Tredgold and Mr. Garfield Todd, and a few others who could oppose the domestic measures and international policies, especially those dealing with Britain. Even in the days of the federation, government spokesmen viewed British control, however tenuous, as alien, and criticism as contemptible. Lord Malvern, the first Prime Minister of the federation, was forthright as usual when he said: "Europeans here are sensible enough not to care two hoots what is said in the British House of Commons. The formula for those in control of the Federation must be: for overseas critics as much contempt as you can; and for our own people, keep the public sweet."[11] Keeping the public sweet meant pursuing policies which enjoyed the full support of the ruling group, and in the federation that meant Rhodesian Europeans.

Meanwhile, the influence of the settler leadership on the African elite has been felt mostly by the traditional rulers, the chiefs. These have largely been compelled, because of their dependence on the government, to serve the latter's interests. But among the modernizing African elite, there has been increasing opposition since the 1958 ouster of Prime Minister Todd, during whose term of office the educated leaders thought that partnership was a realizable ideal. But Todd's party felt that he was going too far too fast and deposed him. Since then, attitudes hardened among both Europeans and Africans.

As noted by a Rhodesian African, B. T. Chidzero, the resistance of the European electorate to political change has stood in the way of moderation among African leaders in multiracial societies: "The only African leader who can impress his followers and arouse the masses is he who bids highest, and the leader who collaborates with Europeans because he is dependent on the European vote soon loses."[12] African leaders can afford to temper their speeches only if they have power; then they can try to win over members from other racial groups. But the ruling minority undermines their position by regarding such leaders as agitators, even Communists, and by taking stern measures to suppress their organizations. Thus the gap between European and African leadership has deepened and widened in Rhodesia.

But for national leaders to operate effectively, a unified system of communications is necessary, in transport as well as mass media. Good roads, trains and air service facilitate quick visits to and contact with distant places; they enable newspapers, books, posters to be delivered quickly and cheaply. As to the media of mass communication, he who controls them can be rightly said to be master of a country. Since both economic and political power are in the hands of the settlers, effective control of all Rhodesian communications is exercised to ensure the preservation of their way of life. After UDI, the government instituted censorship of the press and radio, banned some opposition newspapers and journalists, and in general restricted the circulation, inside and outside Rhodesia, of news detrimental to its interests.

What are the implications of Rhodesia's domestic policies for her international policies? In our view, these fall into two of the categories laid down by Professor Morgenthau: the policies of the status quo and of prestige.

The policy of the status quo is followed by a state (or semistate, in the case of Rhodesia) which wants to retain the power it has.[13] Rhodesia in her attitude toward the British Government, which she regards as meddling in her affairs, has always opposed political changes which threatened the position of the settlers. It is for this reason that the last Prime Minister of the federation, Sir Roy Welensky, accused Britain of bad faith and treachery in his book, *4000 Days* (1965). Thus Rhodesia's close ties with two states pursuing foreign policies of the status quo, South Africa and Portugal, are inevitable. All three are geographically and politically in the same defensive position, and thus help one another. Examples of such help are the supplying of oil to Rhodesia in order to defeat the sanctions applied by Britain. There have also been reports of political refugees from South Africa and South-West Africa being arrested in Rhodesia and sent back to South Africa.[14]

As Morgenthau points out, the aim of the policy of prestige is "to impress other nations with the power one's own nation actually possesses, or with the power it believes or wants the other nations to believe, it possesses."[15] Its instruments are diplomatic, ceremonial display of military force, and propaganda. All three have been widely used by Rhodesia.

After assigning Rhodesia in 1923 her unique status as a virtually independent colony, Britain treated Rhodesia like other independent states enjoying Dominion status within the Commonwealth—through the Commonwealth Relations Office, not the Colonial Office. Further, her Prime Minister was always invited to the annual meetings of the Commonwealth Prime Ministers held in London. Such treatment enhanced her standing and attested to her power not only within the Commonwealth but also outside it, where she could have her own diplomatic representation.

Display of military power has manifested itself first in threats to Britain and to the new African states. As far back as August, 1956, Lord Malvern said in the federal Assembly: "We have complete control of our own Defence Force. I only hope we will not have to use it, as the North American

Colonies had to use it, because we are dealing with a stupid government in the United Kingdom." With the dismantling of the federation, control over the armed forces passed into the hands of the Rhodesian Government, so that this statement could be equally used by Premier Ian Smith. In fact, the UDI was based on the conviction that Rhodesia could stand up against any attack or quell any internal uprising.

Finally, propaganda has been extensively used to present Rhodesia as a country with a stable government, a prospering economy and a reliable ally of the West. One example was a full-page advertisement in *The New York Times* on October 31, 1965, which, among other things, presented Rhodesia as a "strong and determined bulwark against Communist penetration in Africa," and as an oasis of peace and stability in a continent otherwise infested with commotions, corruption and conspiracies. The message in the advertisement was that Rhodesia deserved independence more than the new states in Africa and Asia, now strutting in the councils of the world while they have nothing to boast about except their underdevelopment. This, of course, was an attempt to establish Rhodesia's legitimacy and worthiness as a state. Though contrary to the facts, it was a necessary part of a campaign to create a favorable image and to strike a note that would elicit sympathy for the Smith regime's policies both before and after UDI.

But image-making aside, Rhodesia offers many lessons to Africa, to the community of men.

POSTSCRIPT

RHODESIAN LESSONS*

Power is where power goes.
—President Johnson

Ultimately, the lessons inherent in the Rhodesian situation revolve around power—its use and abuse.

To the major European nation involved, Great Britain, Africans presented a singular and pointed challenge. In protests and demonstrations, both peaceful and violent, Africans charged that Britain, by failing to prevent UDI, had sold their brothers into bondage and had created "another South Africa." For her part, Britain seems to have tried to avoid the mistakes made in South Africa. After the Anglo-Boer War (1899–1902), Britain had sought both to reconcile the defeated Boers with her own kith and kin living in South Africa and simultaneously to promote the interests of the non-Europeans. The administration of Sir Henry Campbell-Bannerman, however, soon found itself in a dilemma which was summarized by G. B. Pyrah:

"To grant unrestricted political freedom to the white races would entail binding the non-whites politically, economically, and socially. To promote the non-Europeans' welfare would alienate the whites, who believed that their political, economic and social status would be undermined thereby."[1]

Britain's response was a policy of reconciliation of Boer and Briton. Concerning the non-Europeans' lot, Churchill, then a Liberal and Under Secretary of State for the Colonies, expressed the hope that "the new charity which may come from that feeling of union may lead the Europeans to unite, not for the purpose of crushing the natives by force, but in the nobler and wiser policy of raising the native to his proper position as an inheritor of what is after all a great estate."[2] As a result, the British government left the now pacified area to follow its own racist policies, laying the foundation for present-day South Africa.

Then, the test of power was in South Africa; today the Africans are convinced that a similar challenge has arisen in Rhodesia. In 1923, Britain gave Rhodesia all effective independence except the "reserved powers" which she has never used to veto discriminating legislation. Indeed, her behavior in the United Nations convinces the Africans that these constitutional powers are nothing but legal fiction—hence the suspicion of complicity in UDI. The suspicion increased after UDI when Britain did not use all possible means to topple the rebel regime. Even when sanctions proved ineffective because South

Africa and Portugal came to the rescue of their stranded neighbor, there was no action. Instead, undenied reports trickled "from well-informed sources" in London and Washington that Britain was "slipping toward a negotiated settlement of the Rhodesian rebellion even if on terms set by Rhodesian Prime Minister, Ian Smith," despite United States coolness to such a move.[3]

The political situation could not but be helpful to the rebels. With the pound sterling wobbling along and the United States fully extended around the globe, no action whatever could be expected from these centers of power. The point is that power went to Salisbury in 1923 and in 1961. The selling out was crowned by the handing of arms to Rhodesia in 1963. To Africa this was South Africa all over again.

While an analogy with South Africa must be treated with care, three points of similarity are particularly significant.

First, the issue in both cases hinges on the fate of the non-Europeans, especially the Africans. Without unfettered control over native affairs the reconciliation of Boer and Briton would have been meaningless—as meaningless as Rhodesia's independence now would be, if Britain had succeeded in laying down conditions for it outside the 1961 Constitution. This is why Mr. Smith insisted on his own terms.

Secondly, constitutional guarantees for the majority's welfare do not work in a state ruled by a racial minority. In South Africa, nothing has stopped the present rulers from whittling down the rights of the non-Europeans. Like Mr. Smith, they are determined to stave off majority rule in their lifetime.

What then of Mr. Smith's "policy of merit," advertised so lavishly in *The New York Times* on October 31, 1965? It fails on two points. First, it assumes that white Rhodesians alone have the God-given right to govern, while Africans have to prove themselves worthy of this right. Despite any protestations to the contrary, such a policy is clearly racial. Second, it assumes that for Rhodesia and Africa the only viable political system is a "democracy on the Western pattern." Experience in Africa's multiracial states disproves this narrow view. Interestingly enough, a delegation of white Kenyans with experience of life in the new African-ruled Kenya was forbidden to enter Rhodesia. Can it be that Mr. Smith's followers do not want their theories disproved, their fears allayed?

Thirdly, it is futile to expect a leader in Mr. Smith's position to reason and compromise. Yet Prime Minister Wilson's negotiations rested on this premise—a premise that betrays either ignorance or wishful thinking in regard to Smith's racist party, the Rhodesian Front. Members of the Front have insisted they will resist to the last rather than be ruled by Africans. For them, African rule means the end of the "most refined political system that civilized man has evolved," and the rise of communism, anarchy or totalitarianism. The *New Statesman* (June 25, 1965) put it succinctly when it said that Mr. Wilson "seems mistakenly to regard Smith as a fundamentally reasonable man with whom, if he is helped to keep the wild men of his party in check, an honorable deal could yet be done."

Seen in terms of a confrontation with power, Rhodesia shows the utter failure of the opposition to act in unison against a common foe. In cases of grave emergency like UDI, opposition operates on two fronts: the moral and the activist. In the former, matters were clear. As early as 1961, the Catholic bishops condemned Rhodesia's racist policies as reminiscent of Nazism—strong words these. When Mr. Smith claimed that through UDI he had struck a blow for the preservation of Christianity, the Anglican Bishop of Mashonaland answered that it was a painful but moral duty for a Christian to oppose an illegal government. Even the use of force was endorsed by no less a figure than the Archbishop of Canterbury, Dr. Ramsey.

But the Front's opponents derived no encouragement from such clear directives. They remained mute as if thunderstruck, as if expecting a blueprint in addition to the moral guidelines. Naturally none came. Still, one can wonder whether in a crisis of this sort a moral solution which is not politically feasible has any use at all. Is there any sense in portraying a desirable distant goal if the mass of the people fail to find their way to it? Or should the masses and their leaders give witness to the moral forces through overt political action? In our view, the question for southern Africa is not *whether* they should be active but *how* more of them should be so. To be sure, there are examples already.

In South Africa, the African National Congress from its inception has had clergymen prominent in its ranks. Henry Ngcayiya, apart from being the first National Chaplain, used his religious contacts as an innocuous means (in the eyes of the rulers) of politicizing African land grievances in Rhodesia. James Calata, Zaccheus Mahabane, John Dube were respectively Secretary-General and Presidents. In Rhodesia, the President of ZANU, Sithole, is also a clergyman.[4]

However, division has always been the bane of African liberation movements. In Rhodesia, political energies were dissipated by the split into ZANU and ZAPU. This disunity, with its concomitant bickering between the two organizations, made it easier for the Front to entrench itself. The ZANU-

ZAPU split merely added a sad chapter to the already distressing story of the southern African liberation movement. It points to a disturbing pattern: as the struggle intensifies, African ranks burst asunder while those of their oppressors become monolithic.

This pattern occurs because power is securely in the hands of the settlers—not in those of a distant metropolitan colonial power, as happened in the rest of Africa. In the latter case, charismatic leaders had the somewhat easier task of rallying mass support for using legal means to impress their nationalist demands on Britain. Fortunately for them, Britain was susceptible to pressures from its own electorate and from its international ties.

As both the Rhodesian and South African struggles show, southern Africa is quite different. Nationalist attempts to make effective use of legal means—boycotts, strikes, demonstrations—strike terror into the ruling whites. In panic, they rush through their parliament increasingly draconian laws to smash the nationalist movements, especially their leaders. The nationalists here face a taxing and unenviable task. To win, they must build mass organizations not dependent on a charismatic leader. In southern Africa, bitter experiences rather than theoretical considerations have thus dictated the need for corporate leadership because of the vulnerabiltiy of an *osagyefo* (redeemer).

Sadly enough, though, such need and futility do not always dawn with equal clarity on the present leaders. Having given all of themselves—their time, comforts and future—they tend (no doubt a human failing) to regard themselves as indispensable and infallible. Thus when differences arise over tactics, they cannot usually be ironed out inside the movement without the leader feeling slighted, insulted and challenged. Hence the splits—beneficial to the ruling group, but dangerous to the cause of liberation.

This danger was immediately apparent to the OAU—hence their constant efforts at reconciling ZANU and ZAPU. Though well intended, these efforts were misdirected and doomed to failure, since the OAU members themselves were split in their support of one or the other group. Two points, arising from Rhodesia but applicable to the whole liberation effort, must be considered by African policy-makers: (1) The OAU itself will have to unite and speak with one voice on Rhodesia or South Africa, and (2) from the liberation movements, each claiming to have the support of the masses at home, the OAU will have to choose just one, and give it full support until it wins or fails.

The case for unity was never more urgent, and it applies to all of Africa, since the liberation is far from over. All the disparate and fractious elements now constituting independent states must derive strength from some form of unity, though it entails sacrifice.

By its nature, power implies such a concentration; diffusion means weakness. The handling of the Rhodesian question by the African states clearly demonstrates the dangers of disunity and weakness. In short, only a strong, united Africa can be a credible threat to the Unholy Alliance of lingering white supremacists and an inspiration to freedom-fighters. Until then, Africans will be confined to rousing rhetorical speeches in the UN, in the OAU, or in Hyde Park. Africa will cajole, threaten, and bluff, but all her efforts will be in vain, however morally unimpeachable her cause.

Here, in the moral approach, Rhodesia has exposed the

weakness of African strategy. The Africans presume that by appealing to the conscience of the West, they will elicit favorable response and action. But they overlook that no State ever acts for somebody else merely out of moral considerations. Africa will have to be a force—a power to be reckoned with—before the world feels compelled to respond to her demands. Power elicits fear and respect from others.

This point emerged with forceful clarity during the Commonwealth Prime Ministers Conference, September 6–15, 1966. Far from making wild, extravagant proposals, President Kaunda of Zambia asked Britain for two reasonable assurances: that a period of direct rule precede the granting of independence to Rhodesia, and that independence be granted only under majority rule. Most of the Afro-Asian members at the Conference took the same line. They reasoned and badgered, but to no avail. In the end, the Conference issued a communique which showed little change in Britain's stand. Urgent though the whole question was, especially for the African Commonwealth members, the communique left Mr. Wilson free to solve the Rhodesian problem in his own manner, and at his own pace.

Basically, there is just one reason for the failure of the Afro-Asian members to achieve their aim: weakness. Long before and, indeed, during the deliberations at Marlborough House, Mr. Wilson knew that the Africans had no strong bargaining position beside their moral approach. Even the threat to quit the Commonwealth cost the Labor Premier no sleepless nights over the prospect of presiding over the dissolution of this organisation often praised as a successful experiment in multiracial living. The threat sounded hollow since Britain stood less to lose, even economically, than the African members.

Indeed, in some British quarters, the prospect of an African walkout was hailed as good riddance. As *The Observer* remarked, there were "many people in Britain and in the 'White Dominions' who would be only too pleased to see the Africans and then the Asians leave the Commonwealth, especially those who are poor or who have awkward problems. Then we could all settle down cosily again with our old kith and kin in an all-white Commonwealth, having washed our hands of some expensive and cantankerous dependents."[5]

Such disenchantment with the Commonwealth as presently constituted appeared in an article published in London in *The Sunday Express* of September 4, 1966, with the appropriately angry title, "It's Time to Kick Out These Blackmailers." Conservative Member of Parliament, Lord Lambton, cited the dissensions among members over Rhodesia and described the Commonwealth as "an association of nations merely based upon idealism without the common philosophy of mutual interests." In other words, for him (as indeed for any realist), idealism must find practical expression in interests commonly pursued by the members. In his view, this was not the case in the new Commonwealth. He, therefore, advised Mr. Wilson to reject very firmly the policies advocated by the Africans on Rhodesia since "the British Government cannot be blackmailed into taking a line directly against the maintenance of peace and the furtherance of its own interests." He also argued for ending the present format of the Commonwealth because it was ridiculous for Britain "to go on paying countless millions a year to countries who return no thanks—only threats and blackmail." Shorn of its polemical trappings,[6] the Lambton article makes one sound point: since the African countries were dependent on handouts from Britain, they had to support the British line on Rhodesia or else quit the Commonwealth and lose vital economic benefits.

The Rhodesian crisis has further fouled and soured the relations between black and white. As the Stanleyville incident showed, today one nasty incident in some obscure and distant part of the world can poison relations among peoples everywhere. Instead of understanding and cooperation, suspicions and dissensions creep in, as is evident in the bitter reaction of Africans to Britain's role in the Rhodesian affair. There is fear of a British "sell-out" to the rebels, with the secret "talks about talks" paving the way to this ignominious ending. President Kaunda's stated reason for not going to the 1966 Commonwealth Conference was his disgust with Mr. Wilson's policy. Another expression of African bitterness was the racialist charge levelled against Wilson by the Zambian Foreign Minister, Simon Kapwepwe.

In brief, the atmosphere prevailing at the Conference was one of distrust of the British Government's sincerity in opposing the Salisbury rebels and seeking their overthrow. One major cause for this distrust was the Wilson proposition that economically Britain could not afford a showdown with South Africa, which was supporting the Smith regime, but that selective sanctions against Rhodesia still could be effective if Britain were given more time to tighten the screws. To the African delegates, the argument was threadbare. Indeed, in the African idiom, it can be described as trying to hide behind a bush that has no leaves. The Conference did not allay these fears and doubts; if anything, it aggravated them.

For Commonwealth Africa, the issue is of particular importance. In those states with substantial multiracial populations, there are fears that Rhodesia may poison race relations that up to now have been generally harmonious. Voices expressing loss of confidence in the Commonwealth ideal have had a racial slant: It was argued that Rhodesia must not be allowed to defy the British government with impunity. For lesser offenses, it was pointed out, Britain did not hesitate to detain or exile the Kabaka, Seretse Khama, Archbishop Makarios and Cheddi Jagan. Why is Britain now reluctant to act in Rhodesia? Why is she refusing to use troops although she has done so in other colonies?

The only answer acceptable to such critics was immediate and strong action. Since the British Government was proving reluctant or unable to forcibly bring down the Front regime, voices from African capitals were heard exhorting the Africans of Rhodesia to take up arms and fight. For example, the Kenya African National Union (KANU), the ruling party in Kenya, urged them "not to wait for others to fight for them. They must be ready to die a little."[7] Such action was urged not only because of UDI but because of the basic injustice of Smith's rule. As *The Observer* (London) put it on October 31, 1965: "The real issue is about power. It is whether the enormous privileges of this minority—both political and economic—shall remain for decades to come. Mr. Smith has not been proposing a declaration of 'independence' but the declaration of a right to racial dictatorship."

Smith declared that right, and in its defence would neither be bullied nor be cowed by outraged Africa. Rhodesia had powerful friends; these gave their powerful support; above all, she, herself, had power. Indeed, the lesson of Rhodesia was a temporary triumph of might over right.

NOTES

INTRODUCTION

[1] Thomas Patrick Melady, *The Revolution of Color* (New York, Hawthorn Books, 1966), p. 30. In this book the author explores in some detail the forces of nationalism among the Afro-Asian peoples, and provides a sound background against which to view the current Rhodesian situation.

CHAPTER I—BEFORE THE SETTLERS CAME

[1] Mr. J. G. Strijdom, Prime Minister of South Africa from 1954 to 1958.

[2] Basil Davidson, "The Fact of African History: an Introduction." *Africa South,* vol. 2, no. 2, January–March 1958, p. 45.

[3] "The Central African Federation," by Sir Roy Welensky in *Africa Speaks,* edited by James Duffy and Robert A. Manners (Princeton, D. van Nostrand Co., 1961), p. 122.

[4] R. N. Hall, *Rhodesia To-day! Its Golden Future! Not Faith, but Facts!* (Rhodesia No. 1, n.d.), p. 1. Available in the New York Public Library.

[5] Howard Hensman, *A History of Rhodesia,* compiled from official sources (Edinburg, W. Blackwood and Sons, 1900), p. 6.

[6] *Old Africa Rediscovered* (London, Gollancz, 1959), p. 207.

[7] P. S. Nazaroff rejects both schools, and gives the credit to the ancient Persians who, he says, settled there. Cf. his article, "What Are the Zimbabwe Ruins—the Solution of Their Secret." *Blackwood's Magazine* (N.Y.), vol. 229, no. 1388, June 1931, pp. 765–792.

[8] The Seshona-speaking Africans are known as the Mashona. But this is a generic term for the Makaranga, Barozwi, Zezuru and other people, who, though culturally distinct, speak a common language.

[9] Roger Summers, "Zimbabwe: Capital of an Ancient Rhodesian Kingdom." *Africa South,* vol. 2, no. 2, January–March 1958, pp. 57–58.

[10] Mongameli Mabona, "Towards an African Philosophy." *Presence Africaine,* vol. 2, no. 30, 1960, pp. 60–61.

[11] See Francisque Marconnes, S. J., "The Karangas." *Nada,* the Southern Rhodesia Native Affairs Department Journal, 1932, p. 14.

[12] H. A. Wieschhoff, *The Zimbabwe-Monomotapa Culture in Southeast Africa.* General Series in Anthropology, no. 8 (Wisconsin, Menasha, George Banta Publishing Company Agent, 1941).

[13] *Ibid.,* p. 102.

[14] Roland Oliver, "Exploring the History of Africa." *Challenge* (Johannesburg), vol. 1, no. 3, May 1964, p. 16.

[15] Quoted in Basil Davidson, *The African Past* (Boston, Little, Brown and Co., 1964), p. 162.

[16] Eric Axelson, *Portuguese in South-east Africa 1600–1700* (Johannesburg, Witwatersrand University Press, 1960), p. 34.

[17] G. R. Boxer, *An African Eldorado: Monomotapa and Mocambique 1498–1752* (Historical Association of Rhodesia and Nyasaland, Local Series No. 2, mimeographed), p. 5.

CHAPTER II—THE CONQUEST OF RHODESIA

[1] J. A. Rogers, *Sex and Race, Negro-Caucasian Mixing in All Ages and All Lands,* vol. I (New York, Rogers, 1940), p. 122.

[2] Lewis H. Gann and Peter Duignan, *White Settlers in Tropical Africa* (Baltimore, Penguin, 1962), p. 32.

[3] Philip Mason, *The Birth of a Dilemma, the Conquest and Settlement of Rhodesia* (London, Oxford University Press, 1958), p. 107.

[4] Quoted in Mason, *ibid.,* p. 105.

[5] J. Kendal, S. J., "King and People." *Nada,* the Southern Rhodesia Native Affairs Department Journal, 1932, p. 96.

[6] Sir Sydney Shippard in a letter to the High Commissioner for South Africa, October 1888. Quoted in Mason, *op. cit.,* p. 122.

[7] "I should offer a steam-boat on Zambesi to King same as Stanley put on the Upper Congo." Rhodes in a letter to Rudd. See *Gold and Gospel in Mashonaland* 1888 (London: Chatto & Windus, 1949), p. 221.

[8] Ronald Robinson and John Gallagher. *Africa and the Victorians, the Climax of Imperialism in the Dark Continent.* (New York, St. Martins Press, 1961). An excellent study.

[9] *Ibid.,* p. 214.

[10] *Ibid.,* p. 221.

[11] Mason, *op. cit.,* p. 128.

[12] Robinson and Gallagher, *op. cit.,* p. 251.

[13] Mason, *op. cit.,* p. 147.

[14] Point Five of the Piet Retief Manifesto. For the complete text see G. W. Eybers, *Select Constitutional Documents Illustrating South African History, 1795–1910* (London, George Routledge & Sons, 1918), pp. 144–145.

[15] R. N. Hall and W. G. Neal, *The Ancient Ruins of Rhodesia* (*Monomotapae Imperium*) (London, Methuen, 1904), p. 121.

[16] John H. Harris, *The Chartered Millions, Rhodesia and the Challenge to the British Commonwealth* (London, Swarthmore Press, 1920), p. 80.

[17] Patrick Keatley, *The Politics of Partnership* (Baltimore, Penguin Books, 1963), p. 167.

[18] *Ibid.*

[19] Elsa Goodwin Green, *Raiders and Rebels in South Africa* (London, George Newnes, 1898), p. 43.

[20] *Ibid.*, p. 44.

[21] Quoted in H. C. Thomson, *Rhodesia and Its Government* (London, Smith, Elder & Co., 1898), p. 234. The letter originally appeared in the *Methodist Times,* January 1897.

[22] White in Thomson, *ibid.*, p. 236.

[23] In a document compiled in the Intelligence Division of the War Office in London in January 1899, Major C. T. Dawkins censored the Administration for its poor intelligence system. He recommended that in time of danger the native policemen and messengers be organized into an Intelligence Department. See his *Precis of Information Concerning Southern Rhodesia* (London, 1899), p. 39.

[24] White in Thomson, *op. cit.*, p. 240.

[25] Point Four of the Manifesto.

[26] The full text of this document can be found in Harris, *op. cit.* pp. 82–83.

[27] Quoted in Harris, *ibid.*, p. 94.

CHAPTER III—RULE BY COMPANY CHARTER

[1] For an excellent discussion of the Jameson Raid, see Jean van der Poel's *The Jameson Raid* (Cape Town, Oxford University Press, 1951). The Raid is relevant for Rhodesia because it contributed to the 1896 uprisings. The Africans were encouraged by the absence of many BSAC troops to attack the settlers.

[2] *Report of the Native Affairs Committee of Enquiry, 1910–11* (Salisbury Government Printer, 1911), p. 25. Sir John Graham was Chairman of the Committee and Herbert S. Keigwin, Secretary.

[3] R. N. Hall, *Rhodesia Today,* pp. 3–4.

[4] BSAC Handbook, *Rhodesia, a Land of Sunshine* (London, April 1921), p. 16.

[5] Harris, *op. cit.*, p. 133. The Africans, the settlers and the British government opposed this claim, and took the matter to the law courts. In 1918 the Privy Council rejected the company's claim, and ruled that since King Lobengula had been defeated the land now belonged to the British Crown, for whom the company was but an agent.

[6] See *Papers Relating to the Southern Rhodesian Native Reserves Commission,* 1915 (London, Her Majesty's Stationery Office, 1917), p. 5, Cd. 8674.

[7] Frank Johnson, "Rhodesia: Its Present and Future." *Journal of the Royal Colonial Institute,* vol. 33, no. 1, Session 1901–1902, p. 26.

[8] See the discussion following Frank Johnson's address, *ibid.*, pp. 28–38.

[9] Quoted in *Report, 1910–11, op. cit.*, p. 30.
[10] *Ibid.*, p. 22.
[11] *Ibid.*
[12] *Ibid.*
[13] *Ibid.*, p. 11.
[14] *Ibid.* p. 2.
[15] *Report of the Education Committee,* 1908. A5–1908 (Salisbury, Argus Printing and Publishing Company, 1908), p. 2.
[16] *Ibid.*, p. 20.
[17] *Report, 1910–11, op. cit.*, p. 13.
[18] *Ibid.*
[19] *Ibid.*, p. 17.
[20] *Ibid.*
[21] H. S. Keigwin. *Report on the Suggested Industrial Development of Natives* (Salisbury, Government Printer, 1920), p. 3.
[22] *Ibid.*

CHAPTER IV—THE END OF COMPANY RULE

[1] For an excellent statement of settler feeling, see her article, "Britain's Youngest Colony." *The National Review* (London), vol. 82, no. 489, November 1923, pp. 447–459; and her book, *The Real Rhodesia* (London, Hutchinson & Son, 1924).
[2] In Ethel Tawse Jollie, *Real Rhodesia,* p. 64.
[3] J. F. Holleman, "Rhodesië in de Stroomversnelling." *Internationale Spectator* (The Hague), vol. 19, no. 22, December 22, 1965, p. 1728.
[4] See her letter in *The Times* (London), October 11, 1965.
[5] *Report of the Chief Native Commissioner for the Year 1919* (Salisbury, Government Printer, 1920), p. 2.
[6] Ken Brown, *Land in Southern Rhodesia* (London, Africa Bureau, 1959), p. 17.
[7] Charles Bullock. *The Mashona and the Matabele* (Cape Town, Juta & Co., 1950), p. 209.
[8] Colin Leys, *European Politics in Southern Rhodesia* (Oxford, Clarendon Press, 1959), p. 31.
[9] Ethel Tawse Jollie, "Southern Rhodesia, a White Man's Country in the Tropics." *The Geographical Review* (New York), vol. 17, no. 1, January 1927, p. 89.

CHAPTER V—THE RISE OF AFRICAN NATIONALISM

[1] For this point on the role of the Mlimu-Mwari religion I am heavily indebted to Dr. T. O. Ranger, now of the University College, Dar es Salaam, for his two well-researched papers, *The Organization of the Rebellions of 1896 and 1897,* Parts 1 and 2, presented at the Conference of the History of the Central African Peoples—the 17th conference of the Rhodes-Livingstone Institute for Social Research, May 28–June 1, 1963 (Lusaka).

[2] Quoted in Ranger, *ibid.*, Part 1: "The Rebellion in Matabeleland," p. 20.

[3] George Shepperson and Thomas Price, *Independent African,* John Chilembwe and the Origin, Setting and Significance of the 1915 Nyasaland Native Uprising (Edinburgh, Edinburgh University Press, 1958), pp. 70–71.

[4] Quoted in Shepperson and Price, *ibid.*, p. 76.

[5] See W. S. Taberer's *Reports for the Years 1901–3* (Salisbury, Argus Printing & Publishing Company).

[6] See T. O. Ranger, *Traditional Authorities and the Rise of Modern Politics in Southern Rhodesia: 1898–1930.* Paper presented to the Conference of the History of the Central African Peoples, 17th Conference of the Rhodes-Livingstone Institute for Social Research, May 28–June 1, 1963 (Lusaka), p. 3.

[7] See Ranger, *ibid.*, pp. 5–7.

[8] See *Report of the Chief Native Commissioner for Matabeleland for 1912,* p. 6, and *Report of the Chief Native Commissioner for the Years 1915 and 1919.*

[9] Ranger, *op. cit.*, p. 5.

[10] See A. J. B. Hughes, *Kin, Caste and Nation among the Rhodesian Ndebele.* The Rhodes-Livingstone Papers, No. 25 (Manchester, Manchester University Press, 1956), p. 78.

[11] *Report for the Year 1910* (Salisbury, Government Printer, 1911), p. 1.

[12] *Report of the Chief Native Commissioner for the Year 1919, op. cit.,* p. 1.

[13] Ranger, *op. cit.*, p. 9.

[14] Quoted in Ranger, *op. cit.*, p. 11.

[15] Mary Benson, *The African Patriots,* the Story of the African National Congress of South Africa (Chicago, Encyclopaedia Britannica Press, 1964), p. 49.

[16] Quoted in Ranger, *op. cit.*, p. 13.

[17] Quoted in Nathan Shamuyarira, *Crisis in Rhodesia* (London, Andre Deutsch, 1965). See pp. 30–31 for a full statement of its aims and objects.

[18] J. van Velsen, "Trends in African Nationalism in Southern Rhodesia," *Kroniek van Afrika* (Leiden), vol. 4, no. 2, June 1964, p. 141.

[19] J. F. Holleman, *op. cit.*, p. 1731.

[20] Quoted in Ranger, *op. cit.*, p. 16.

[21] N. Shamuyarira, *op. cit.*, p. 34.

[22] J. van Velsen, *op. cit.*, p. 143.

[23] Ndabaningi Sithole, *African Nationalism* (Cape Town, Oxford University Press, 1959), p. 20.

[24] Sithole, *ibid.*, pp. 155–156.

[25] Quoted in Boris Gussman, *Out in the Mid-day Sun* (New York, Oxford University Press, 1963), p. 71.

CHAPTER VI—THE RISE OF THE FEDERATION

[1] For most of these statistics, see "Tightening the Screws on Rebellious Rhodesia," *Business Week* (New York), November 20, 1965, pp. 40–41.

[2] *Time,* November 5, 1965, p. 42.

[3] Boris Gussman, *op. cit.,* pp. 115, 117.

[4] *Memorandum on Native Policy in East Africa* (London, HMSO, 1930), Cmd. 3573.

[5] *Report of the Commission on Closer Union of the Dependencies in Eastern and Central Africa* (London, HMSO, 1929), Cmd. 3234.

[6] Margery Perham, "The Rhodesian Crisis: the Background." *International Affairs* (London), vol. 42, no. 1, January 1966, p. 5.

[7] For a short but excellent study of the background, issues and personalities involved in the federation movements, see Kenneth Kirkwood, "British Central Africa: Politics under Federation." *The Annals,* vol. 298, March 1955, pp. 130–141.

[8] *Rhodesia-Nyasaland Royal Commission, Report* (London, HMSO, 1939), Cmd. 5949, p. 215.

[9] *Ibid.,* p. 218.

[10] Robert I. Rotberg, *The Rise of Nationalism in Central Africa,* the Making of Malawi and Zambia, 1873–1964 (Cambridge, Harvard University Press, 1965), p. 215.

[11] *Ibid.,* p. 223.

[12] Arthur Creech Jones, "British Colonial Policy with particular reference to Africa." *International Affairs* (London), vol. 27, no. 2, April 1951, pp. 181–182.

[13] Roy Welensky, "Toward Federation in Central Africa." *Foreign Affairs,* vol. 31, no. 1, October 1952, pp. 142–149.

[14] *Ibid.,* p. 143.

[15] *Ibid.,* p. 148.

[16] Shamuyarira, *op. cit.,* pp. 15–16.

[17] *Ibid.,* p. 18.

[18] For this party's program, see T. R. M. Creighton, *The Anatomy of Partnership,* Southern Rhodesia and the Central African Federation (London, Faber & Faber, 1960), pp. 193–198.

[19] Cf. *The Economist,* December 19, 1953, p. 874.

CHAPTER VII—THE FALL OF THE FEDERATION

[1] Enoch Dumbutshena, "Southern Rhodesia Explodes." *Africa South in*

[2] R. S. Garfield Todd, "The Only Turning." *Ibid.,* pp. 71–72.

[3] Lawrence C. Vambe, "An African looks at Federation." *African Affairs,* vol. 58, no. 233, October 1959, p. 288.

CHAPTER VIII—THE GATHERING STORM OVER UDI

[1] For its stormy life, see Shamuyarira, *op. cit.,* Chapter 4.

[2] *Keesings Historisch Archief* (Amsterdam), October 12, 1962, p. 367.

[3] Shamuyarira, *op. cit.,* p. 74.

[4] *Time,* December 21, 1962.

[5] See "Upheaval in Central Africa." *The New Republic,* December 29, 1962, p. 5.

[6] For this point, see the writer's article, "The Crisis in Rhodesia." *America,* December 4, 1965.
[7] See Shamuyarira, *op. cit.,* Chapter 10, for an account of the split.
[8] *Keesings Historisch Archief, op. cit.,* May 1, 1964, p. 268.
[9] The People's Caretaker Council (PCC) was founded by Nkomo to continue the work of ZAPU, banned at home but functioning abroad. For the sake of clarity, we are throughout this book using the name ZAPU.

CHAPTER IX—RHODESIA AND THE UNITED NATIONS

[1] *Yearbook of the United Nations, 1964.* (United Nations, Office of Public Information, 1966), p. 444.
[2] Sir Hugh Foot, *A Start in Freedom* (London, Hodder and Stoughton, 1964).
[3] "U.S. Policy on Rhodesia." *Africa Report,* February, 1966.
[4] *South Africa Bulletin,* No. 5, March 1966 (New York, American Committee on Africa).
[5] *The Christian Science Monitor,* March 19, 1966.
[6] See *De Nieuwe Rotterdamse Courant,* November 15, 1965.

CHAPTER X—AFRICA VERSUS WHITE RHODESIA

[1] For PAFMECA principles, see A. J. Hughes, *East Africa: the Search for Unity, Kenya, Tanganyika, Uganda and Zanzibar* (Baltimore, Penguin, 1963), p. 230.
[2] The major goal of PAFMECA was to unite these areas after indepence into an economic (and perhaps eventually) political union. Cf. the speech by Mbiyu Koinange of Kenya, Secretary-General, in Lusaka, November 21, 1962 (*Keesing's Contemporary Archives,* January 19–26, 1963), p. 19206.
[3] Quoted by Colin Legum in Britannica, *Book of the Year 1964* (Chicago, Encyclopaedia Britannica, Inc., 1964), p. 100.
[4] Cf. *Keesing's Contemporary Archives, op. cit.,* June 12–22, 1963, p. 19464.
[5] For the full text of the Joint Memorandum by Representatives of African Liberation Movements, see *Addis Ababa Summit,* 1963 (Addis Ababa Ministry of Information, 1963), pp. 92–93.
[6] In Accra, October, 1965, the Assembly added Zambia and Somalia—hence the new name "Committee of Eleven."
[7] Shamuyarira, *op. cit.,* Chapter 10.
[8] *Africa and the World* (London), No. 11, August 1965, pp. 9–14.
[9] Cf. *Africa Report,* August 1965, p. 30.
[10] Shamuyarira, *op. cit.,* p. 190.
[11] *The Reporter,* vol. 4, no. 138, July 30, 1965, p. 15.
[12] *Spotlight on South Africa* (Dar es Salaam, African National Congress of South Africa, May 21, 1965).
[13] For text, see *Africa Report,* December 1965, p. 36.
[14] Cf. *The New York Times,* October 24, 1965.
[15] Excerpts in *West Africa,* January 15, 1966, p. 65.

[16] December 12, 1965. From now on, this newspaper will be referred to as the *NRC.*

[17] For details on the improbability of the OAU military intervention, see J. H. Huizinga in the *NRC,* November 25 and 30, 1965; *De Groene Amsterdammer,* November 20, 1965; and *The New York Times,* December 7, 1965.

[18] *Newsweek,* November 29, 1965.

[19] Quoted in *Africa Institute Bulletin* (Pretoria), vol. 4, no. 1, January 1966, p. 16, and in *The Reporter,* December 3, 1965, p. 14.

[20] *The New York Times,* December 4, 1965.

[21] *West Africa,* December 11, 1965, p. 1397.

[22] Julius Nyerere, "Why I am threatening to break with Britain." *The Observer* (London), December 12, 1965.

[23] Cf. *The New York Times,* December 13 and 24, 1965.

[24] *Ibid.,* December 19, 1965.

[25] *Ibid.,* December 17, 1965.

[26] *The Times* (London), January 12, 1966.

[27] *Ibid.,* March 3, 1966.

[28] *The New York Times,* March 5, 1966.

[29] Dean Acheson, *A Citizen Looks at Congress* (New York, Harper & Brothers, 1957), p. 120.

CHAPTER XI—UDI AND THE RACE QUESTION

[1] Colin Legum, *Pan-Africanism, a short political guide* (London, Pall Mall Press, 1962), p. 33.

[2] *Ghana*—Press Release No. 3, October 18, 1965 (New York, Ghana Information Services).

[3] Rosalynde Ainslie, *The Unholy Alliance—Salazar, Verwoerd and Welensky* (London, Anti-Apartheid Movement, 1962).

[4] See *Statements on Southern Rhodesia by the President and Government of Ghana,* October 1965 to January 1966 (Accra, Publicity Secretariat, Ministry of Foreign Affairs, n.d.), p. 7.

[5] In *West Africa,* November 20, 1965, p. 1321.

[6] John Hargreaves, "Pan-Africanism After Rhodesia." *World Today,* February, 1966, p. 60.

[7] See *West Africa, op. cit.*

[8] Julius K. Nyerere, "Rhodesia in the Context of Southern Africa." *Foreign Affairs,* vol. 44, no. 3, April 1966, pp. 373–386.

[9] *Ibid.,* p. 378.

[10] Gwendolen M. Carter, "Rhodesia—Embattled Frontier of Africa's White Redoubt." *Northwestern Review,* vol. 1, no. 2, February, 1966, p. 26.

[11] *Michigan Chronicle,* December 4, 1965.

[12] *Atlanta Daily World,* December 25, 1965.

[13] Text in the *Atlanta Daily World, ibid.*

[14] R. C. Pratt, "African Reactions to the Rhodesian Crisis." *International Journal* (Toronto), vol. 21, no. 2, Spring, 1966, pp. 186 ff.

CHAPTER XII—A STATE BUT NOT A NATION

[1] Quoted in *The Observer* (London), May 1, 1966.

[2] See "Secretary Dulles discusses U.S. Foreign Policy for British Television Broadcast" (transcript of interview). *Department of State Bulletin,* vol. 39, no. 1011, November 1958, p. 735.

[3] Mill, *Considerations on Representative Government* (Chicago, Henry Regnery Co., 1962), p. 307. This Gateway edition, a reprinting of the original published in 1861, is introduced by Professor F. A. Hayek.

[4] *Ibid.*

[5] Quoted in French by the Foreign Minister of The Netherlands, J. M. A. Luns, in his "Independence or Interdependence." *International Affairs* (London), vol. 40, no. 1, January 1964, p. 1.

[6] Mill, *op. cit.,* p. 4.

[7] Philip Mason, *op. cit.,* p. 181.

[8] *The Times* (London), March 31, 1938.

[9] Waldemar A. Nielsen, *African Battleline: American Policy Choices in Southern Africa* (New York, Harper & Row, 1965), p. 41.

[10] Margery Perham, "The Rhodesian Crisis: the Background." *International Affairs* (London), vol. 42, no. 1, January 1966, p. 3.

[11] Quoted in Keatley, *op. cit.,* p. 387.

[12] B. T. G. Chidzero, "African Nationalism in East and Central Africa." *International Affairs* (London), vol. 36, no. 4, October 1960, p. 474.

[13] Hans J. Morgenthau, *Politics among Nations, the Struggle for Power and Peace,* 3rd edition (New York, Alfred A. Knopf, 1965), p. 39.

[14] See *A Survey of Race Relations in South Africa,* 1962, compiled by Muriel Horrell (Johannesburg, South African Institute of Race Relations, 1963), pp. 225–226.

[15] Morgenthau, *op. cit.,* p. 73.

POSTSCRIPT—RHODESIAN LESSONS

* The author is grateful to the publishers of *America,* the National Catholic Weekly Review, for permission to incorporate material which appeared in the edition of December 4, 1965.

[1] G. B. Pyrah, *Imperial Policy and South Africa 1902–1910,* (Oxford, Clarendon Press, 1955), p. 87.

[2] *Ibid.,* p. 103.

[3] *New York Herald Tribune* (European edition), August 5, 1966. See also *De Telegraaf* (Amsterdam) of the same date.

[4] The ruling groups have had two clergymen as Prime Ministers of Rhodesia and South Africa respectively: Todd and Malan.

[5] *The Observer* (London), September 4, 1966. See also *The New York Times,* October 2, 1966.

[6] The basic flaw in Lord Lambton's argument is that he regards the Commonwealth as a static "old boys' club," not a dynamic organization capable of adjusting to changing times and needs.

[7] Cf. *Kenya Digest* (London, Kenya High Commission), August 19, 1966.

THE POLITICS OF SOUTHERN AFRICA 1960–1966

A Selective Bibliography

PREFACE

This bibliography aims at bringing together the literature on the politics of Southern Africa from 1960 to mid-1966. To handle the vast amount of literature on this area requires selection. My selection is governed by one rule: namely, to include material representing as wide a range of views as possible. For this reason, I have not hesitated to list items from earlier periods that I thought relevant.

For my purpose, Southern Africa comprises Angola, Mozambique, Rhodesia, the Republic of South Africa, South West Africa, and the former High Commission Territories—Basutoland, Bechuanaland, and Swaziland.

For allowing me to use their facilities, I thank the Library of Congress, the New York Public Library, and the libraries of these universities: Chicago, Harvard, Howard, and Northwestern.

TABLE OF CONTENTS

1. SOUTHERN AFRICA

General

AINSLIE, ROSALYNDE. "Southern African Alliance," *World Today,* Vol. 21, No. 7, July 1965, pp. 276–278.

———. *The Unholy Alliance: Salazar, Verwoerd, Welensky.* London: Anti-Apartheid Movement, 1962. Shows economic and military cooperation among South Africa, Portugal, and Rhodesia.

AWUYE, SYLVESTER W. K. *South Africa and Portuguese Territories: A Study in African Diplomacy in the United Nations.* Master's dissertation, University of Chicago, 1964, 141 pp. Explains tactics of African states in the U.N. concerning South Africa, South West Africa, and Portuguese-speaking Africa.

BRZEZINSKI, ZBIGNIEW (ed.). *Africa and the Communist World.* Stanford: Stanford University Press, 1963, 272 pp. Covers Communist activities in Southern Africa.

COWEN, D. V. *The Foundations of Freedom.* Capetown: Oxford University Press, 1961, 258 pp. Detailed discussion of natural law as the basis of government, with special reference to Southern Africa.

———. *Liberty, Equality, Fraternity—Today.* Johannesburg: South African Institute of Race Relations, 1961, 35 pp. Case for government based on natural law.

De Blij, Harm J. *Africa South.* Evanston: Northwestern University Press, 1962, 399 pp. A geographer presents issues facing Southern Africa.

Du Bois, W. E. Burghart. *The World and Africa,* New York: International Publishers, 1965, 352 pp. An inquiry into the part which Africa has played in world history; an enlarged edition with new writings on Africa, 1955–1961, particularly relevant to Southern Africa.

Ferkiss, Victor C. *United States Policy in Southern Africa.* Paper read at the Fourth International Conference, Howard University, Washington, D.C., April 11–13, 1963, 18 pp. mimeographed. Characterizes policy as negative, having only marginal effects on Southern Africa.

Gann, Lewis H., and Duignan, Peter. *White Settlers in Tropical Africa.* Baltimore: Penguin Books, 1962, 170 pp. Historians state the settlers' case.

Good, Robert C. "Africa's Unfinished Struggle for Freedom: The Real Issues," *Department of State Bulletin,* Vol. 47, No. 1224, December 10, 1962, pp. 882–887. U.S. official points out problems in new states and in Southern Africa.

Howe, Russell Warren. "Showdown in Southern Africa: Sequel to Rhodesian Sanctions," *New Leader,* February 28, 1966.

Kotze, J. C. G. *Principle and Practice in Race Relations According to Scripture.* Stellenbosch: S.C.A. Publishers, 1962, 156 pp. Critical examination of the Bible.

Kuper, Hilda. "The Colonial Situation in Southern Africa," *Journal of Modern African Studies,* Vol. 2, No. 2, July 1964, pp. 149–164. Considers social relations between Africans and whites.

Marais, Ben. *The Two Faces of Africa,* Pietermaritzburg: Shuter and Shooter, 1964, 205 pp. Arguments for and against apartheid, alternatives, impact of ideology and religion on new African states.

Mason, Philip. *Race Relations in Africa.* London: SCM Press, 1960, 24 pp. A plea for open-mindedness.

Melady, Thomas Patrick. "The Sweep of Nationalism in Africa," *Annals Amer. Acad. Political and Social Sci.,* Vol. 354, July

1964, pp. 91–96. Argues that unless there is international intervention, violence will erupt in South Africa, Rhodesia, and territories under Portuguese rule.

———. *The White Man's Future in Black Africa.* New York: Macfadden, 1962, 208 pp. Plea for white men to accept change in the new Africa.

MOLNAR, THOMAS. *Africa: A Political Travelogue.* New York: Fleet Publishing Corporation, 1965, 304 pp. Favors Portuguese policies; is impressed by Rhodesian and South African views.

NIELSEN, WALDEMAR A. *African Battleline: American Policy Changes in Southern Africa.* New York: Harper & Row, 1965, 155 pp. Southern African issues and their implications for the United States.

QUIGG, PHILIP W. (ed.). *Africa—A Foreign Affairs Reader.* New York: Praeger, 1964, 346 pp. Selection of articles from *Foreign Affairs,* many dealing with Southern Africa.

RICHMOND, ANTHONY H. *The Colour Problem. A Study of Racial Relations.* Baltimore: Penguin Books, 1961, 374 pp. Sociological analysis of racial problems in British areas, including those in Southern Africa.

SCHUMANN, T. E. W. *The Abdication of the White Man.* Cape Town: Tafelberg-Vitgevers. 1963, 189 pp. The white man has a special mission in Africa.

United States Senate Committee on Foreign Relations. "United States Foreign Policy—Africa," Study No. 4, in *United States Foreign Policy,* Document No. 24. Washington, D.C.: Government Printing Office, 1961, pp. 301–390.

WALKER, ERIC A. (ed.). *The Cambridge History of the British Empire,* Vol. VIII, "South Africa, Rhodesia, and the High Commission Territories." Cambridge: University Press, 1963, 1087 pp. Southern Africa from ancient times to 1921.

WELENSKY, ROY. "The United Nations and Colonialism in Africa," *Annals Amer. Acad. Political and Social Sci.,* Vol. 354, July 1964, pp. 145–152. Accuses U.N. of using double standards in Africa.

WILLSON, F. M. G. "Prospects for Southern Africa," *Current History,* March 1966.

2. FORMER HIGH COMMISSION TERRITORIES

General

ANONYMOUS. "The Protectorates," *The Afro-Asian Journalist,* Vol. 2, No. 3, May–June 1965, pp. 38–39, 63–65.

ASHTON, E. H. "Protectorates in South Africa," *New Society,* Vol. 2, No. 57, October 31, 1963, pp. 11–13. Shows dilemma based on past and future of these territories; doubts practicality of independence.

BULL, THEODORE. "The Problem Protectorates," *World Today,* Vol. 19, No. 11, November 1963, pp. 491–498.

COCKRAM, BEN. "The Protectorates—An International Problem," *Southern Africa,* January 3, 1964, pp. 10–11. Predicts independence, since these territories are unlikely to accept Bantustan plan.

DOXEY, G. V. *The High Commission Territories and the Republic of South Africa.* London: Oxford University Press, 1963, 51 pp. A "Chatham House Memorandum" which brings up to date developments in these territories and their relations with South Africa.

Great Britain. *Basutoland, Bechuanaland Protectorate, and Swaziland* (Report of an economic survey mission). London: H.M. Stationery Office, 1960, 555 pp. Study of political and economic conditions (Morse Report).

GREAVES, L. B. *The High Commission Territories: Basutoland, the Bechuanaland Protectorate, and Swaziland.* London: Edinburgh House Press, 1954, 24 pp. History, economic and social development; relations with Great Britain and South Africa.

G.V.D. "Recent Developments in the High Commission Territories," *World Today,* Vol. 18, No. 1, January 1962, pp. 17–23. Political and economic developments.

HAILEY, LORD. *The Republic of South Africa and the High Commission Territories.* London: Oxford University Press, 1963, 136 pp. Relations with South Africa and future of these territories.

HALPERN, JACK. *South Africa's Hostages, Basutoland, Bechuanaland, and Swaziland.* Hammondsworth: Penguin African Library, 1965, 496 pp. Shows dependence of these territories on South Africa; offers practical suggestions for helping them.

MARQUAND, HILARY. "The High Commission Territories," *Africa South in Exile,* Vol. 4, No. 4, July–September 1960. Territories seen from Labour party viewpoint.

MAUD, JOHN. "The Challenge of the High Commission Territories," *African Affairs,* Vol. 63, No. 251, April 1964, pp. 94–103.

NKOANA, MATTHEW. "Persecution or Sanctuary: Will the British Labour Government Allow Collusion Between Verwoerd and the High Commission Territories Police?" *The New African,* Vol. 4, No. 4, June 1965, pp. 77–78. Accuses Territories Police of cooperating with South African Police to stop opponents.

ORCHARD, R. K. *The High Commission Territories of South Africa.* London: World Dominion Press, 1951, 35 pp. Relates British acquisition of these territories and missionary work there.

RUBIN, LESLIE. "The High Commission Territories: What Now?" *Africa Report,* Vol. 9, No. 4, April 1964, pp. 9–10.

SPENCE, J. E. "British Policy Towards the High Commission Territories," *Journal of Modern African Studies,* Vol. 2, No. 2, July 1964, pp. 221–246. Careful assessment of the question of whether Britain neglected these territories because of their uncertain future.

STEVENS, RICHARD P. *The Transkei Bantustans and the High Commission Territories.* Paper read at the National Conference on the South African Crisis and American Action, Washington, D.C., March 21–23, 1965, 12 pp. mimeographed. Examines territories in terms of fulfilling Bantustan plan.

TAVERNE, D. *The Unprotected Protectorates: Basutoland, Bechuanaland, Swaziland.* London: Fabian Society, 1965, 25 pp.

Lesotho (Formerly Basutoland)

ANONYMOUS. "Basutoland Realities," *Southern Africa,* May 8, 1964, p. 323. Urges independence for Basutoland.

———. "Political Development in Basutoland," *International Bulletin of the Africa Institute,* Vol. 11, No. 3, March 1964, pp. 69–83. History, party programs, and new constitution.

BASUTOLAND CONGRESS PARTY. *Basutoland Petitions the United Nations, May 1962.* Cairo: Basutoland Congress Party, External Mission, 1962, 67 pp. Petition urging immediate independence.

DUNCAN, PATRICK. "Basutoland in Transition," *Africa South,* Vol. 3, No. 3, April–June 1959, pp. 55–59. Reaction to Moore Report.

GREAT BRITAIN. *Basutoland Constitutional Conference.* London: H.M. Stationery Office, 1964, 16 pp. Conference report on last constitution before independence.

ROTBERG, ROBERT. "Basutoland—1962," *Africa Report,* Vol. 7, No. 2, February 1962, pp. 9*ff*.

STEVENS, RICHARD P. "Basutoland: Vigorous Nationalism in a Stagnant Economy," *Africa Report,* Vol. 9, No. 4, April 1964, pp. 11–13.

WELCH, CLAUDE E., JR. "Zambia and Lesotho: The Transfer of Power," *Africa Report,* Vol. 9, No. 6, June 1964, pp. 10–11. A comparative study in constitutional problems.

Botswana (Formerly Bechuanaland)

ANONYMOUS. "Verwoerd's Bechuanaland?" *The New African,* Vol. 4, No. 2, April 1965, p. 26. Significance of 1965 election; urges British aid.

BENSON, MARY. *Tshekedi Khama.* London: Faber and Faber, 1960, 318 pp. Biography of Seretse Khama's uncle.

GREAT BRITAIN. *Bechuanaland Constitutional Proposals.* London: H.M. Stationery Office, 1964, 13 pp. Proposals forming the basis of new government structure.

KHAMA, TSHEKEDI. *Bechuanaland, A General Survey.* Johannesburg: South African Institute of Race Relations, 1957, 36 pp.

———. *Bechuanaland and South Africa.* London: African Bureau, 1955, 20 pp. Plea for independence, not transfer of Bechuanaland to South Africa.

MUNGER, EDWIN S. *Bechuanaland: Pan-African Outpost or Bantu Homeland?* London: Oxford University Press, 1965, 114 pp. Bechuanaland's development and external relations.

RENSBURG, PATRICK VAN. "Bechuanaland the Coveted Liability," *The New African,* Vol. 4, No. 2, April 1965, pp. 32–34; Vol. 4, No. 3, May 1965, pp. 67–68. Describes economic developments, relations with South Africa, and problems for independent Bechuanaland.

STEVENS, RICHARD P. "Bechuanaland: The Reconciliation of Traditional and Modern Forces," *Africa Report,* Vol. 9, No. 4, April 1964, pp. 15–17.

Swaziland

ANONYMOUS. "Political Developments in Swaziland," *International Bulletin of the Africa Institute,* Vol. 11, No. 4, April 1964, pp. 119–133. History, constitutions, party programs, position of Europeans.

COWEN, D. V. *Swaziland.* Report on constitutional reform, made on behalf of the Swaziland Progressive Party and the Eurafrican (Colored) Welfare Association. Swaziland Progressive Party, 1961, 34 pp.

KUDER, HILDA. *The Swazi, A South African Kingdom.* New York: Holt, Rinehart & Winston, 1963, 87 pp. Analysis of Swazi society and implications of change for the future.

LASHINGER, M. "Roads to Independence: The Case of Swaziland," *World Today,* Vol. 21, No. 11, November 1965, pp. 486–494.

STEVENS, RICHARD P. "Report from Swaziland," *African Report,* Vol. 8, No. 9, October 1963, p. 8.

———. "Swaziland: A Constitution Imposed," *Africa Report,* Vol. 9, No. 4, April 1964, pp. 13–15.

———. "Swaziland Political Development," *Journal of Modern African Studies,* Vol. 1, No. 3, September 1963, pp. 327–350. Analyzes interaction between South Africa, Britain, and Swazi political groups.

WELCH, CLAUDE E., JR. "Constitution Confusion in Swaziland," *Africa Report,* Vol. 8, No. 4, April 1963, pp. 7–9.

3. PORTUGUESE-SPEAKING TERRITORIES

General

AWUYE, SYLVESTER W. K. (See under Southern Africa—General.)

DUFFY, JAMES. *Portugal in Africa.* Cambridge: Harvard University Press, 1962, 240 pp. History and policy of Salazar.

———. "Portugal in Africa," *Foreign Affairs,* Vol. 39, No. 3, April 1961, pp. 481–493. States policies and Portuguese resistance to change.

———. *Portugal's African Territories: Present Realities.* New Carnegie Endowment for International Peace, 1962, 39 pp. Analysis of 1960–1961 events and opposition groups.

EVANGELISTA, JULIO. *Portugal vis-à-vis the United Nations.* Lisbon, 1961, 78 pp. Report by the Six and Convention 107; denies the existence of Portuguese colonies under Article 73 of the U.N. Charter.

FIGUEIREDO, ANTONIO DE. *Portugal and Its Empire: The Truth.* London: Gollancz, 1961, 159 pp. Attack on Portuguese colonial policies.

GALVAO, HENRIQUE. *Santa Maria: My Crusade for Portugal.* New York: World Publishing Co., 1961, 261 pp. Seizure of the ship *Santa Maria;* includes Galvao's report and an appendix on Portuguese colonies.

MARTELLI, GEORGE. "Portugal and the United Nations," *International Affairs,* Vol. 40, No. 3, July 1964, pp. 453–465. Shows how Portugal argues in the U.N. that she has no colonies.

MOREIRA, ADRIANO. *Portugal's Stand in Africa.* New York: University Publishers, 1962, 265 pp. Addresses by a Cabinet Minister and texts of 1961 colonial decrees.

SILVA CUNHA, J. M. DA. "Political Aspects of the New Africa," *African Affairs,* Vol. 63, No. 253, October 1964, pp. 270–280. Portugal's African policy in relation to African nationalism, Pan-Africanism, Communism.

WOHLGEMUTH, P. "The Portuguese Territories and the United Nations," *International Conciliation,* No. 545, November 1963. Shows U.N.'s difficulties in treating these territories.

United Nations Special Committee on Territories under Portuguese Administration. *General Policies in Territories under Portuguese Administration.* Background paper prepared by the Secretariat. New York: United Nations, 1963, 53 pp., U.N. Document A/AC 108/L7.

Angola

ANDRADE, MARIO DE. "Angolan Nationalism," *Presence Africaine,* Vol. 14/15, No. 42/43, 1962, pp. 7–23. View of the President of the Popular Movement for the Liberation of Angola (MPLA).

Anonymous. *Angola: A Symposium.* London: Oxford University Press, 1962, 160 pp. Views on 1961 revolt by Portuguese government missionaries, opposition groups.

BARDEN, A. K. "Some Aspects of Portuguese Imperialism and the National Liberation Movements in Angola and Mozambique," *The Pan-Africanist Review* (Accra), Vol. 1, No. 3, September 1964, pp. 62–74.

DAVIDSON, BASIL. "Angola 1961, the Factual Record," *Presence Africaine,* Vol. 10, No. 38, 1962, pp. 5–25.

EHNMARK, ANDERS, and WASTERG, PER. *Angola and Mozambique: The Case Against Portugal.* New York: Roy, 1964, 176 pp.

HOUSER, GEORGE M. *Nationalist Organizations and Leaders in Angola: Status of the Revolt.* Paper read at the Fourth International Conference, Howard University, Washington, D.C., April 11–13, 1963, 28 pp. mimeographed.

JACK, HOMER A. *Angola: Repression and Revolt in Portuguese Africa.* New York: American Committee on Africa, 1960, 28 pp. Foreshadows the 1961 revolt.

LARCIER, HENRI. "The Union of the Angolese Populations (U.P.A.)," *Presence Africaine.* Vol. 14/15, No. 42/43, 1962, pp. 37–43. Describes policy of opposition group led by Roberto Holden.

MAHALA, C. "Portugal and the Colonies of Angola and Guinea," *Presence Africaine,* Vol. 2, No. 30, 1960, pp. 14–28. Attacks Portuguese administration.

MARCUM, JOHN. "The Angola Rebellion: Status Report," *Africa Report,* Vol. 9, No. 2, February 1964, pp. 3–7. Shows policies and activities of opposition groups.

MARTELLI, GEORGE. "The Future in Angola," *African Affairs,* Vol. 61, No. 245, October 1962, pp. 300–307. Denies existence of internal opposition.

NKRUMAH, KWAME. "Angola," *Presence Africaine,* Vol. 14/15, No. 42/43, pp. 24–36. President of Ghana attacks Portuguese administration.

Portuguese-American Committee on Foreign Affairs. *The Communists and Angola.* Boston, no date. Committee views unrest in Angola as "part of the international Communist conspiracy, a part of the plan to destroy the United States itself."

TEIXEIRA, BERNARDO. *The Fabric of Terror. Three Days in Angola.* New York: Devin-Adair, 1965, 176 pp. Describes outbreak and significance of violence in 1961.

Mozambique

BARDEN, A. K. "Some Aspects of Portuguese Imperialism and the National Liberation Movements in Angola and Mozambique," *The Pan-Africanist Review,* Vol. 1, No. 3, September 1964, pp. 62–74.

EHNMARK, ANDERS, and WASTBERG, PER. *Angola and Mozambique: The Case Against Portugal.* New York: Roy, 1964, 176 pp.

MAHALA, C. "The Horror of Mozambique," *Africa South in Exile,* Vol. 5, No. 1, October–December 1960, pp. 50–59.

MONDLANE, EDUARDO C. "The Movement for Freedom in Mozambique," *Presence Africaine,* Vol. 25, No. 53, 1965, pp. 8–37. Portuguese rule and rise of African opposition told by President of the Mozambique Liberation Front (FRELIMO).

———. *The Struggle for Independence in Mozambique.* Paper read at the Fourth International Conference, Howard University, Washington, D.C., April 11–13, 1963, 26 pp. mimeographed.

MUNGER, EDWIN S. "Mozambique: Uneasy Today, Uncertain Tomorrow. Comments on Portugal's African Territory," *American Universities Field Staff Reports Service* (Central and South African Series), Vol. 9, No. 4, 1961, 19 pp. Shows factors creating unrest.

WHEELER, DOUGLAS L. *The Portuguese and Mozambique: The Past Against the Future.* Paper read at the Fourth International Conference, Howard University, Washington, D.C., April 11–13, 1963, 24 pp. mimeographed.

4. REPUBLIC OF SOUTH AFRICA

AFRICAN NATIONAL CONGRESS. *The African National Congress.* Dar es Salaam: African National Congress of South Africa, 1963, 24 pp. Policies of African National Congress, opposition from Pan-Africanist Congress.

ANONYMOUS. "The People Unconquerable, South Africa after Rivonia," *The African Communist,* No. 18, July–September 1964, pp. 3–16. Significance of Rivonia Trial.

ANONYMOUS. "Profile," *Black Star* (London), Vol. 1, No. 1, May 1963, pp. 1–4. Describes work of Pan-Africanist Congress leader Sobukwe.

ANONYMOUS. "South Africa," *Bulletin of the International Commission of Jurists,* No. 22, April 1965, pp. 35–43. Study of restrictions on movements and residence of Africans.

AVERINK, ANNIE. "Nee tegen de Apartheid," *Politick en Cultuur* (Amsterdam), Vol. 25, No. 1, January 1965, pp. 23–29. A Marxist-Leninist analysis.

AWUYE, SYLVESTER W. K. (See under Southern Africa—General.)

AZAD, SAVITRI. "How Vorster Uses Anti-Communism," *The African Communist,* No. 20, January–March 1965, pp. 54–64. How fear of communism is used to silence opponents of government policies.

BALLINGER, RONALD B. *South Africa and the United Nations: Myth and Reality.* Johannesburg: South African Institute of International Affairs, 1963, 32 pp. Hostility to South Africa is not confined to Afro-Asian states; discusses disputes between U.N. and South Africa.

BEER, Z. J. DE. *Multi-Racial South Africa: The Reconciliation of Forces.* London: Oxford University Press, 1961, 69 pp. Opposing views of Afrikaner nationalists and Africans can be reconciled through a qualified franchise advocated by Progressive party.

BELLWOOD, W. A. *Whither the Transkei?* London: Bailey Bros. & Swinfin, 1964, 124 pp. Author favorably impressed with potentialities and personalities in the new Bantu state, but sees difficulty.

BENSON, MARY. *South Africa: The Struggle for a Birthright.* Hammondsworth: Penguin African Library, 1966, 314 pp. History of African National Congress till 1965 as told by an admirer.

———. *On Trial for their Lives—The Accused at Rivonia.* London: African Bureau, 1964, 13 pp. Text of a statement delivered before the United Nations Special Committee on the Policies of Apartheid of the Government of the Republic of South Africa on March 11, 1964. Sets forth political views of the accused and pleads for action against apartheid.

BERGHE, PIERRE L. VAN DEN. *South Africa, A Study in Conflict.* Middletown: Wesleyan University Press, 1965, 371 pp. A sociologist shows sources of conflict and evaluates government, ideology, and social institutions as reflecting apartheid.

BRETT, E. A. "How South Africa's Africans React," *New Society* (London), No. 61, November 28, 1963, pp. 6–8. Opinion survey of 1961 of middle class Africans shows 43 percent believe violence is inevitable.

BROUGHTON, MORRIS. *Press and Politics of South Africa.* Cape Town: Purnell, 1961, 306 pp. Analysis of interaction between press and politics.

BROWN, WILLIAM O. *Race Relations in the American South and in South Africa.* Boston: Boston University Press, 1959, 23 pp. A comparison of backgrounds, realities, and trends.

BUNTING, BRIAN. *The Rise of the South African Reich.* Hammondsworth: Penguin African Library, 1964, 332 pp. South Africa's racial policies compared to those of the Nazis.

———. *The Story Behind the Non-European Press—Who Runs Our Newspapers?* Cape Town: New Age, 1959, 9 pp. Non-

European press cannot speak for non-Europeans because it is controlled by big business.

CALLAN, EDWARD. *Albert John Luthuli and the South African Race Conflict*. Kalamazoo: Western Michigan University Press, 1962, 75 pp. Luthuli's role as a mediator.

CALVOCORESSI, PETER. *South Africa and World Opinion*. London: Oxford University Press, 1961, 68 pp. World reaction to apartheid; failure to exert pressure on South Africa.

CARTER, GWENDOLEN N. "African Nationalist Movements in South Africa," *The Massachusetts Review*, Vol. 5, No. 1, Autumn 1963, pp. 147–164. ANC and PAC analyzed in terms of their appeal to Africans.

———. "The Consequences of Apartheid," *Annals Amer. Acad. Political and Social Sci.*, Vol. 306, July 1956, pp. 38–42. Considers economic factors.

———. *The Politics of Inequality: South Africa Since 1948*. New York: Praeger, 1958, 535 pp. Studies of politics of all groups in South Africa.

CHURCHILL, RHONA. *White Man's God*. New York: Morrow, 1962, 205 pp. Apartheid examined from the standpoint of missionaries and religion.

COWEN, D. V. *Constitution-Making for a Democracy, An Alternative to Apartheid*. Johannesburg: Anglo American Corporation of South Africa, 1960, 41 pp. Supplement to *Optima*, March 1960. Proposes a new constitution to remove racial tensions and to safeguard against abuse of power.

———. *Freedom of Thought and Its Expression in South Africa*. Cape Town: National Union of South African Students, 1960, 30 pp. A philosophical case for free thought and expression, which are curtailed in South Africa.

DUNCAN, PATRICK. "Is Apartheid an Insoluble Problem?" *Race*, Vol. 6, No. 4, April 1965, pp. 263–266. Uses Algerian experience to show that it is too late to keep the mass of the white population in South Africa.

———. *South Africa's Rule of Violence*. London: Methuen, 1964, 139 pp. Description of violence and cruelty resulting from apartheid.

———. "Toward a World Policy for South Africa," *Foreign Affairs*, Vol. 42, No. 1, October 1963, pp. 38–48.

FAGAN, H. A. *Co-Existence in South Africa.* Cape Town: Juta, 1963, 125 pp. Advocates government through effective consultation between ruling whites and nonwhites.

FEIT, EDWARD. *South Africa: The Dynamics of the African National Congress.* London: Oxford University Press, 1962, 73 pp. Reasons for ANC's ineffectiveness.

FOURIE, SCHEEPERS. "Across the Colour Line, Some Remarks on South African Writing," *The African Communist,* No. 19, October-December 1964, pp. 77–85. Examines how South African writers treat race question.

FRASER, DONALD M. "American Policy Toward South Africa," *Congressional Record,* Appendix (89th Congress, 1st Session), Vol. 3, No. 53, March 24, 1965, pp. A1378–1380. A congressman urges change in policy.

GINIEWSKI, PAUL. *Bantustans, A Trek Towards the Future.* Cape Town: Human & Rousseau, 1961, 257 pp. Regards Bantustans as a solution to race problem.

GONZE, COLLIN; HOUSER, GEORGE M.; and STURGES, PERRY M. *South African Crisis and United States Policy.* New York: American Committee on Africa, 1962, 63 pp. U.S. involvement in supporting present regime.

GRAAFF, DE VILLIERS. "South African Prospect, Thoughts on an Alternative Race Policy," *Foreign Affairs,* Vol. 39, No. 4, July 1961, pp. 670–682. Leader of United party states party policies.

GUINGAND, FRANCES DE. "South Africa in Perspective," *Perspective,* Vol. 2, No. 7, April 1965, pp. 14–15. Defends South Africa, valuable partner to the West.

HATCH, JOHN. "South African Crisis in the Commonwealth," *Journal of International Affairs,* Vol. 15, No. 1, 1961, pp. 68–76. South African racial policies and reaction in the Commonwealth.

HIGGINS, ROSALYN. "South Africa's Standing in International Organizations," *World Today,* Vol. 19, No. 12, December 1963, pp. 507–511. Shows attempts to exclude South Africa from international organizations.

HILL, CHRISTOPHER R. *Bantustans: The Fragmentation of South Africa.* London: Oxford University Press, 1964, 112 pp. Merits and demerits of Bantustan plan.

HOLLOWAY, JOHN E. "Apartheid," *Annals Amer. Acad. Political and Social Sci.,* Vol. 306, July 1956, pp. 26–37. Apartheid explained by South African Ambassador to U.S.A.

HORRELL, MURIEL. *A Decade of Bantu Education.* Johannesburg: South African Institute of Race Relations, 1964, 186 pp.

———. *Action, Reaction and Counteraction.* Johannesburg: South African Institute of Race Relations, 120 pp. A review of nonwhite opposition to the apartheid policy, countermeasures by the government, and the eruption of new waves of unrest.

———. *Legislation and Race Relations.* Johannesburg: South African Institute of Race Relations, 1963, 68 pp. A summary of the main South African laws which affect race relationships.

HURLEY, DENIS. *Apartheid: A Crisis for the Christian Conscience.* Johannesburg: South African Institute of Race Relations, 1964, 22 pp.

HUTCHINSON, ALFRED. *Road to Ghana.* London: Gallancz, 1960, 190 pp. Experiences of a treason trial suspect and his escape to Ghana.

INTERNATIONAL COMMISSION OF JURISTS. *South Africa and the Rule of Law.* Geneva: International Commission of Jurists, 1960, 239 pp. Apartheid examined in terms of its violation of the rule of law.

KARIS, THOMAS. "The South African Treason Trial," *Political Science Quarterly,* Vol. 76, No. 2, 1961, pp. 217–240. Origin, course, and political significance of the trial.

KENNEDY, JOSEPH P. *American Private Involvement in South Africa.* Paper read at the National Conference on the South African Crisis and American Action, Washington, D.C., March 21–23, 1965, 25 pp. mimeographed. Shows that U.S.A. supports apartheid through tourism, sports, entertainment, and exchange programs.

KUNENE, RAYMOND. "The End of Non-Violence: 2. A Tactic Not a Doctrine," *The New African,* Vol. 4, No. 1, March 1965, pp. 4–7. ANC view on post-Sharpeville developments.

KUPER, LEO. *An African Bourgeoisie—Race, Class and Politics in South Africa.* New Haven: Yale University Press, 1965, 452 pp. A politicosociological study showing that the professional African's high occupational status and low civic status make for violence.

———. "Racialism and Integration in South African Society," *Race,* Vol. 4, No. 2, May 1963, pp. 26–31.

LANDIS, ELIZABETH S. "South African Apartheid Legislation: I. Fundamental Structure; II. Extension, Enforcement, and Perpetuation," *Yale Law Journal,* Vol. 71, No. 1, November 1961, pp. 1–52; Vol. 71, No. 3, January 1962, pp. 437–500. Legal framework and major laws examined.

LAWRIE, G. G. "South Africa's World Position," *Journal of Modern African Studies,* Vol. 2, No. 1, March 1964, pp. 41–54.

LEBALLO, POTLAKO. "Pan Africanist Congress Fully Supports Second Bandung Confab," *The Afro-Asian Journalist* (Djakarta), Vol. 2, No. 3, May–June 1965, pp. 41–47. Policy statement by Acting President of PAC.

LEGUM, COLIN and MARGARET. *South Africa: Crisis for the West.* London: Pall Mall, 1964, 333 pp. Intervention by the West and the U.N. as the only way to peaceful change.

LEWIN, JULIUS. *Politics and Law in South Africa: Essay on Race Relations.* London: Merlin, 1963, 115 pp. South Africa analyzed by a liberal.

LOUW, ERIC H. *The Case for South Africa, As Put Forth in the Public Statements of Eric H. Louw.* New York: MacFadden, 1963, 189 pp. Addresses to U.N. General Assembly by the Foreign Minister, in which he defends policies of his government.

LUTHULI, A. *Freedom Is the Apex.* Johannesburg: South African Congress of Democrats, no date, 8 pp. ANC President states aims of African struggle.

———. *Let My People Go, An Autobiography.* Johannesburg: Collins, 1962, 256 pp.

MABHIDA, MOSES. *For International United Action to End Apartheid, the Curse of South Africa.* London: W.F.T.U. Publications, 1961, 48 pp. A trade unionist attacks apartheid.

MALHOTRA, RAM C. "Apartheid and the United Nations," *Annals Amer. Acad. Political and Social Sci.,* Vol. 354, July 1964, pp. 135–144. Rapporteur of the U.N. Special Committee on Apartheid analyzes U.N.'s search for a peaceful solution.

MANNING, CHARLES A. W. "In Defense of Apartheid," *Foreign Affairs,* Vol. 43, No. 1, October 1964, pp. 135–149. Apartheid defended as the philosophy of patriots.

MARAIS, BEN. *The Two Faces of Africa.* (See under Southern Africa—General.)

MARQUARD, LEOPOLD. *The Peoples and Policies of South Africa.* London: Oxford University Press, 1960, 247 pp. Introductory guide.

MBEKI, GOVAN. *South Africa: The Peasants' Revolt.* Hammondsworth: Penguin African Library, 1964, 159 pp. Shows opposition in Transkei to Bantustan plan.

MEZERIK, A. G. (ed.). *Apartheid in the Republic of South Africa: Bantustans, Boycotts, U.N. Action.* New York: International Review Service, Vol. 10, No. 82, 1964, 109 pp. Apartheid since 1960; resolutions passed by international organizations—U.N., O.A.U.

MILLER, D. J. B. "South Africa's Departure," *Journal of Commonwealth Political Studies,* Vol. 1, 1961–1963, pp. 56–71. Commonwealth Prime Ministers' Meeting of 1961 and deliberations leading to South Africa's departure from the Commonwealth.

MKELE, NIMROD. "The Effects of Apartheid," *New Society,* Vol. 2, No. 46, August 15, 1963, pp. 6–7. Harmful effects on urban Africans.

MODISANE, BLOKE. *Blame Me on History.* New York: Dutton, 1963, 311 pp. Autobiography by an African; portraying life for a black man in South Africa.

MULLER, HILGARD. "Separate Development in South Africa," *African Affairs* (London), Vol. 62, No. 246, January 1963, pp. 53–63. Address by South African Ambassador to Britain.

MUNGER, EDWIN S. *Notes on the Formation of South African Foreign Policy,* Pasadena: Castle Press, 1965, 102 pp. Evaluates institutions and individuals who formulate foreign policy.

NEAME, L. E. *A History of Apartheid: The Story of the Colour War in South Africa.* London: Pall Mall, 1962, 200 pp. Arguments for and against apartheid.

NGUBANE, JORDAN K. *An African Explains Apartheid.* New York: Praeger, 1963, 243 pp. Shows policies of Liberals, Communists, ANC, and PAC in fighting apartheid.

NKOANA, MATTHEW. "The End of Non-Violence: 1. First Phase of an Unfolding Programme," *The New African,* Vol. 4, No. 1, March 1965, pp. 3–6. PAC representative regards 1960 as first step.

———. "The Epic of Sharpeville: Before and After—An Assessment," *The Afro-Asian Journalist,* Vol. 2, No. 2, March–April 1965, p. 17. PAC policy and views of background to Sharpeville.

NKOSI, LEWIS. "Robert Sobukwe: An Assessment," *Africa Report,* Vol. 7, No. 4, April 1962, pp. 7–9. Assesses stature and work of PAC President.

NOKWE, DUMA. "Congress and the Africanists. 2. Congress Replies," *Africa South,* Vol. 4, No. 3, April–June 1960, pp. 33–38. ANC reply to PAC views (in the same edition, pp. 24–32).

OLIVIER, N. J. J. *Ons Stedelike Naturellebevolking.* Johannesburg: Suid-Afrikaanse Uitsaaikorporasie, 1959, 24 pp. Government policy and work for Africans in urban areas.

PATON, ALAN. "Liberals Reject Violence," *Liberal Opinion,* Vol. 3, No. 4, October 1964, pp. 1–4. President of Liberal party rejects use of violence by members.

PIENAAR, S., and SAMPSON, ANTHONY. *South Africa: Two Views of Separate Development.* London: Oxford University Press, 1960, 81 pp. Pienaar gives the government's view, Sampson that of a liberal.

PIERSON-MATHY P. (compiler). "Apartheid in Zuid-Afrika," *Internationale Spectator* (The Hague), Vol. 19, No. 13, July 8, 1965, pp. 1004–1120. Whole edition devoted to theory, application of apartheid. Includes section on African opposition.

PLESSIS, WENTZEL C. DU. *Highway to Harmony: A Report on Relationships in South Africa.* New York: Information Service of South Africa, 1958, 28 pp. South Africa's Ambassador to the U.S.A. explains his government's policies.

QUIGG, PHILIP W. *South Africa: Problems and Prospects* (with commentary by J. S. F. Botha, Kenneth Carstens, Vernon

McKay). New York: Council on Religion and International Affairs, 1965, 48 pp. Different views on South African politics.

RABOROKO, P. NKUTSOEU. "Congress and the Africanists: (1) The Africanist Case," *Africa South,* Vol. 4, No. 3, April–June 1960, pp. 24–32. PAC view.

REEVES, AMBROSE. *South Africa—Yesterday and Tomorrow: A Challenge to Christians.* London: Gollancz, 1962, 173 pp.

RENSBURG, PATRICK VAN. *Guilty Land, the History of Apartheid.* New York: Praeger, 1962. History and political views of government, United Party Progressives, Liberals, ANC, PAC.

RHOODIE, N. J., VENTER, H. J. *Apartheid, a Socio-historical Exposition of the Origin and Development of the Apartheid Idea.* Cape Town: H.A.U.M., 1959, 268 pp. Supporters of apartheid explain development of South African whites' views on color and resulting idea and policy of apartheid.

ROBERTS, MARGARET. "Poqo," *World Today,* Vol. 19, No. 7, July 1963, pp. 279–282. Origin and role of Poqo and its relation to PAC.

ROSKAM, K. L. *Apartheid and Discrimination.* Leyden: Sythoff, 1960, 179 pp. Remarks with regard to the relationship between white and respective nonwhite ethnic groups in the Union of South Africa. Apartheid found lacking a scientific and moral basis.

ROUX, EDWARD. *Time Longer than Rope—A History of the Black Man's Struggle for Freedom in South Africa.* Madison: University of Wisconsin Press, 1964, 469 pp. History of South Africa seen from the side of the black man.

RUBIN, LESLIE and NEVILLE. *This Is Apartheid.* London: Christian Action, 1965, 16 pp. Forty-five examples of South Africa's racial laws.

SABLONIERE, MARGRIT DE. *Apartheid.* Amsterdam: Querido, 1960, 125 pp. Implications of apartheid for black and white South Africans; appendix of historical documents.

SACHS, E. S. *The Anatomy of Apartheid.* London: Collet's, 1965, 424 pp. Role played by financiers inside and outside South Africa.

SANDOR (pseudonym). *The Coming Struggle for South Africa.* London: Fabian Society, 1963, 36 pp. Analysis of forces fighting in South Africa and of Britain's stake in the struggle.

SCOTT, MICHAEL. "The Essential Duplicity of Apartheid," *Presence Africaine,* Vol. 2, No. 30, 1960, pp. 3–13.

SEGAL, RONALD (ed.). *Sanctions Against South Africa.* Hammondsworth: Penguin African Library, 1964, 272 pp. Papers presented to the International Conference on Ecomomic Sanctions against South Africa, London, 1964. Economic sanctions found practical, legal, and necessary.

SHAH, K. K. "British Democracy and Economic Sanctions Against South Africa," *Africa Quarterly* (New Delhi), Vol. 4, No. 1, April–June 1964, pp. 4–8. Urges Britain to apply sanctions.

SISULU, WALTER. "Congress and the Africanists," *Africa South,* Vol. 3, No. 4, July–September 1959, pp. 27–34. ANC member discusses relations with PAC.

SPENCE, J. E. *Republic Under Pressure, A Study of South African Foreign Policy.* London: Oxford University Press, 1965, 132 pp. Describes probable effects of external pressures on South African government; South Africa's relations with African states.

———. "Tradition and Change in South African Foreign Policy," *Journal of Commonwealth Political Studies,* Vol. 1, 1961–1963, pp. 136–152.

STANILAND, MARTIN. "Apartheid and the Novel, Desperation and Stoicism in a Situation which Frustrates," *The New African,* Vol. 4, No. 1, March 1965, pp. 15–17.

STEVENS, RICHARD P. *The Transkei, Bantustans and the High Commission Territories.* (See under High Commission Territories—General.)

SWORD OF THE SPIRIT. *The Church to Africa—Pastoral Letters of the African Hierarchies.* London: Sword of the Spirit, 1960, 136 pp. Statements from 1952 to 1958 by Roman Catholic bishops, including three on apartheid.

TABATA, I. B. *Education for Barbarism, Bantu Education in South Africa.* Durban: Prometheus, no date. Attack on government's education policy for Africans.

TAMBO, OLIVER. "Apartheid—The Indictment," *The Pan-Africanist Review* (Accra), Vol. 1, No. 2, 1964, pp. 29–40. Apartheid as seen by an ANC official.

TATZ, C. M. "Dr. Verwoerd's 'Bantustan' Policy," *Australian Journal of Politics and History,* Vol. 8, No. 1, May 1962, pp. 7–26. Solutions not accepted by Africans stand little chance of success.

TRAPIDO, STANLEY. "Political Institutions and Afrikaner Social Structures in the Republic of South Africa," *American Political Science Review,* Vol. 57, No. 1, March 1963, pp. 75–87. Economic, religious, and educational institutions make South African political system so rigid that Afrikaners cannot make concessions to English-speaking whites and nonwhites.

UNITED NATIONS. General Assembly Special Committee on the Policies of Apartheid of the Government of the Republic of South Africa. *Report,* addendum. New York: United Nations, 1963, 169 pp. U.N. Document A/5497/Add. 1.

———. Office of Public Information. *A New Course in South Africa,* New York: United Nations, 1964, 35 pp. U.N. experts favor national convention representing all South Africans to chart a new course.

VERWOERD, H. F. *Bantu Education:* Policy for the Immediate Future. Pretoria: Department of Native Affairs, 1954.

———. *The Price of Appeasement in Africa.* Pretoria: South African Information Service, 1960.

WALSHE, A. P. "The Changing Content of Apartheid," *The Review of Politics,* Vol. 25, No. 3, July 1963, pp. 343–361. Shows shift in ideas of different leaders.

WILSON, MONICA. "The Early History of the Transkei and Ciskei," *African Studies* (Johannesburg), Vol. 18, No. 4, 1959, pp. 167–179. Evidence from Portuguese records showing that Nguni-speaking people were in South Africa in the sixteenth and seventeenth centuries.

WOLLHEIM, O. D. "The Coloured People of South Africa," *Race,* Vol. 5, No. 2, October 1963, pp. 25–41. Legislation estranging coloreds from whites.

YEOWART, WILLIAM S. "Sanctions and Boycotts," *Perspective* (London), September 1964, pp. 5–8. Opposes sanctions and boycotts.

5. SOUTH WEST AFRICA

ANONYMOUS. "South-West Africa," *The African Communist,* No. 18, July–September 1964, pp. 21–27. Analysis of Odendaal Report.

ANONYMOUS. "South West Africa," *International Bulletin* (Africa Institute), Vol. 11, No. 5, May 1964, pp. 137–168. Whole issue is devoted to this territory; discusses form of government, geography, economy, international status, Odendaal Report.

ANONYMOUS. "Towards The Hague," *Southern Africa,* January 31, 1964, pp. 79–80. Supports South African claim to South West Africa.

AWUYE, SYLVESTER W. K. (See under Southern Africa—General.)

BALLINGER, RONALD B. *South West Africa: The Case Against the Union.* Johannesburg: South African Institute of Race Relations, 1961, 58 pp.

EMANUEL, P. A. "De Inwoners van Zuidwest-Afrika en hun welzijn," *Internationale Spectator,* Vol. 19, No. 10, May 22, 1965, pp. 854–867. White inhabitants of South West Africa support administration by South Africa; Africans oppose but are divided.

GINIEWSKI, PAUL. "SWA and the International Court," *Perspective* (London), Vol. 2, No. 8, May 1965, pp. 3–6. Considers South Africa's proposal that ICJ visit South West Africa; separate development policy in South West Africa supported by local inhabitants.

GOLDBLATT, ISIDOR. *The Mandate Territory of South West Africa in Relation to the United Nations.* Cape Town: Struik, 1961, 67 pp. Position of South West Africa from the League of Nations to the United Nations.

JANDOVIC, BRANIMIR M. "International Legal Aspect of the Problem of South-West Africa," *Africa Quarterly,* Vol. 4, No. 3, October–December 1964, pp. 179–191.

KERINA, MBURUMBA. *South West Africa—Past, Present, and Future.* Paper read at the Fourth International Conference,

Howard University, Washington, D.C., April 11–13, 1963, 35 pp. mimeographed. Discusses Good Offices Committee, jurisdiction of the International Court of Justice, and the role of the United States.

KOZONGUIZI, JARIRETUNDU. *The Historical and Legal Status of South West Africa.* Paper read at the Fourth International Conference, Howard University, Washington, D.C., April 11–13, 1963, 10 pp.

LANDIS, ELIZABETH S. "South West Africa in the International Court of Justice," *Africa Today,* Vol. 11, April 1964, pp. 10–12.

LEVINSON, OLGA. *The Ageless Land, The Story of South West Africa.* Cape Town: Tafelberg-Uitgewers, 1961, 151 pp. Describes country and its development by Germans and South Africans.

LOWENSTEIN, ALLARD K. *Brutal Mandate, A Journey to South West Africa.* New York: Macmillan, 1962, 257 pp. Experiences in South West Africa and South Africa.

MASON, PHILIP. "Separate Development and South West Africa; Some Aspects of the Odendaal Report," *Race,* Vol. 5, No. 4, April 1964, pp. 83–97. Uses political and historical comparisons to study report and race relations.

MUNGER, EDWIN S. "South-West Africa: Evolution or Revolution?" *American Universities Field Staff, Reports Service* (Central and Southern Africa Series), Vol. 9, No. 6, 1961, 16 pp.

RAALTE, E. VAN. "De Rechtsstrijd over Zuid-West Afrika," *Internationale Spectator,* Vol. 19, No. 5, March 8, 1965, pp. 325–338. Historical survey of legal struggle.

RENSBURG, H. M. JANSE VAN. *Die Internasionale Status van Suidwes-Afrika: 'n kritiese beskouing van die Internasionale Hof van Justisie se Raadgevende Mening van 11 Julie 1950.* Leiden: "Luctor et Emergo," no date, 154 pp. History and legal analysis of the Mandate, showing that South Africa alone can terminate the Mandate.

SCOTT, MICHAEL. *The Orphans' Heritage, The Story of the South West African Mandate.* London: Africa Bureau, 1958, 24 pp. Argues that the problem goes beyond international law.

———. *South West Africa: Political Parties and Nationalist Demands.* Paper read at the Fourth International Conference,

Howard University, Washington, D.C., April 11–13, 1963, 29 pp. mimeographed.

STEWARD, ALEXANDER. *The Sacred Trust—South West Africa.* Johannesburg: Da Gama Publications, 1963, 46 pp. A general introduction, inclined to support South Africa's administration.

UNION OF SOUTH AFRICA. *South West Africa and the Union of South Africa: The History of a Mandate.* New York: South African Government Information Service, no date, 108 pp. Proves that African inhabitants favor incorporation of South West Africa into South Africa.

YANKSON, J. ACKAH. *South West Africa in the International Scene.* 1953, 24 pp. Argues through international law that South Africa is holding South West Africa illegally.

6. SOUTHERN RHODESIA

ANONYMOUS. "Southern Rhodesia, Constitutional Future," *Africa Institute Bulletin,* Vol. 11, No. 7, July 1964, pp. 211–215. Developments under Winston Field, Smith.

ANONYMOUS. "U.N. Spotlight on Southern Rhodesia," *World Today,* Vol. 18, No. 11, November 1962, pp. 456–459. U.N. handling of Southern Rhodesia as a colonial question.

AUSTIN, DENNIS. "Sanctions and Rhodesia," *World Today,* Vol. 22, No. 3, March 1966, pp. 106–113.

BROWN, RICHARD. "Zambia and Rhodesia: A Study in Contrast," *Current History,* Vol. 48, No. 284, April 1965, pp. 201–206. Shows political differences.

BULL, THEODORE. "Politics and Power in the Rhodesias," *World Today,* Vol. 18, No. 7, July 1962, pp. 274–279.

———. "Two Views of the Central African Federation: II. The Situation in Southern Rhodesia," *World Today,* Vol. 19, No. 7, July 1963, pp. 311–316.

CABLE, M. "We and They in Rhodesia," *The New Yorker,* February 19, 1966.

CHIDZERO, B. T. G. "African Nationalism in East and Central Africa," *International Affairs,* Vol. 36, No. 4, October 1960, pp. 464–475.

CREIGHTON, T. R. M. *The Anatomy of Partnership, Southern Rhodesia and the Central African Federation.* London: Faber & Faber, 1960, 258 pp. Southern Rhodesia's culture and its influence on the Federation's race relations.

FRANCK, THOMAS M. *Southern Rhodesian Nationalism in the East Central African Conflict.* Paper read at the Fourth International Conference, Howard University, Washington, D.C., April 11–13, 1963, 52 pp. mimeographed. Analyzes problems and prospects of African nationalism.

GANN, L. H. *A History of Southern Rhodesia,* to 1934. London: Chatto & Windus, 1965, 354 pp.

——— and GELFAND, M. *Huggins of Rhodesia: The Man and His Country.* London: Allen & Unwin, 1964, 285 pp. Biography of first Prime Minister, champion of the settlers' cause.

GIBBS, PETER. *Avalanche in Central Africa.* London: Barker, 1961, 169 pp. Describes race relations giving rise to unrest.

HALPERN, JACK. "Rhodesian Reflections," *New Society,* No. 68, January 16, 1964, p. 23. Blames "lack of human contact between white and black" for troubles.

HASSON, R. H. "Rhodesia—A 'Police State'?" *World Today,* Vol. 22, No. 5, May 1966, pp. 181–190. Shows systematic rejection of legal standards since the 1950's.

HIRSCH, M. I. *Focus on Southern Rhodesia: The Constitution and Independence.* Bulawayo: Stuart Manning, 1964, 64 pp. Supports 1961 Constitution.

HOOD, M. "Rhodesia and Portugal; The Unholy Alliance," *New Statesman,* February 26, 1965.

KLEIN, G. "Rhodesia and the World's Conscience," *Christian Century,* February 2, 1966.

LAVIN, DEBORAH. "The Republic and the Rebel," *World Today,* Vol. 22, No. 3, March 1966, pp. 89–92. Points out clandestine help by South Africa.

LEYS, COLIN. *European Politics in Southern Rhodesia.* Oxford: Clarendon Press, 1959, 323 pp.

MARKARIS, JOHN. "African versus European in Central Africa," *Journal of International Affairs,* Vol. 15, No. 1, 1961, pp. 52–67.

M'KABE, DAVIS B. C. "Rhodesia: State of Emergency," *Africa Today,* Vol. 12, No. 2, February 1965, pp. 10–12.

MNYANDA, B. J. *In Search of Truth: A Commentary on Certain Aspects of Southern Rhodesia's Native Policy*. Bombay: Hind Kitabs, 1954, 173 pp. Commentary on politics, education, and economics.

NKOMO, JOSHUA. "The Case for Majority Rule in Southern Rhodesia," *Africa Quarterly,* Vol. 4, No. 2, July–September 1964, pp. 90–101. Views of the President of the Zimbabwe African People's Union (ZAPU).

PALLEY, C. *The Constitutional History and Law of Southern Rhodesia, 1885–1965* (with special reference to Imperial control). Oxford: Clarendon Press, 1966, 872 pp.

PARKER, F. "Rhodesia in Crisis," *Negro History Bulletin,* December 1965.

SEGAL, AARON. "Rhodesia: What Next?" *Africa Report,* Vol. 10, No. 5, May 1965, pp. 23–24. Describes war of nerves between Rhodesia and Britain.

SHAMUYARIRA, N. M. "The Coming Showdown in Central Africa," *Foreign Affairs,* Vol. 39, No. 2, January 1961, pp. 291–298. Foreshadows breakup of Federation because of racial policies as exemplified by Southern Rhodesia.

SMITH, I. D. "Southern Rhodesia and Its Future," *African Affairs,* Vol. 63, No. 250, January 1964, pp. 13–22. Discusses the economy and independence.

STOKES, ERIC. "The Southern Rhodesian Tangle," *New Society,* No. 89, June 11, 1964, pp. 6–8. Background to conflict.

UNITED NATIONS. General Assembly, Special Committee on the Situation with Regard to the Implementation of the Declaration on the Granting of Independence to Colonial Countries and People. *Report: Southern Rhodesia.* New York: United Nations, 1963, U.N. Documents A/5446/Add. 3.

WALSHE, A. P. "Rhodesia: Backdrop to Crisis," *Africa Report,* Vol. 9, No. 10, November 1964, pp. 12–16. Political developments since breakup of Federation.

WHITEHEAD, EDGAR. "Southern Rhodesia," *International Affairs,* Vol. 36, No. 2, April 1960, pp. 188–196. Prime Minister states his government's policy.

WILLIAMS, G. MENNEN. "Southern Rhodesia Today," *Department of State Bulletin,* July 12, 1965.

INDEX

THE AUTHOR AND HIS BOOK

BENEDICT VULINDLELA MTSHALI, a South African Zulu, is a specialist in Pan-African affairs, particularly in regard to southern Africa, and has close contacts with the nationalist movements and leaders in the area.

He has studied at Pius XII College in Basutoland, the University of Nijmegen and the Institute of Social Studies, both in the Netherlands, and at Fordham University in New York, earning graduate degrees in journalism, social science and political science. His articles have appeared in various publications here and abroad.

Mr. Mtshali is currently working on a Ph.D. degree in political science at New York University.

RHODESIA: BACKGROUND TO CONFLICT was set in type, printed and bound by American Book–Stratford Press, Inc., New York City. The text and chapter heads were set in Times Roman, a type face designed by Stanley Morison in 1932 for the newspaper *The Times* of London. Medium in weight and simple in design, Times Roman offers a high degree of legibility and beauty.

A HAWTHORN BOOK